HARMONIC

My Story of a Living Harmonic Form

DR. ALEXANDRA PORTER, PH.D

Copyright © 2025 by Dr. Alexandra Porter, PH.D.

ISBN 978-1-965390-07-8 (softcover)
ISBN 978-1-965390-08-5 (hardcover)

All rights reserved. No part of this book may be reproduced or transmitted in any form or by any means, electronic or mechanical, including photocopying, recording, or by any information storage and retrieval system without express written permission from the author, except in the case of brief quotations embodied in critical reviews and certain other noncommercial uses permitted by copyright law.

Printed in the United States of America.

CONTENTS

Union from Divine Energy 3

Law of Group Consciousness 11

The Stranger, a Voice, That Process 24

The Tingling Family..34

The Water Pond 49

Me And the Power of Tingling 57

I Could Have Sworn I Heard the Birds Cry.......................65

"Me" Forgets Who "We" Are..80

Universal Energy 87

Divine Essence Always Lights the Darkness.....................103

The Vehicle of the Ego 137

The Green Daffodils 151

FOREWORD

My mother once said that in this world, spirituality was "routine" for those who dedicated their lives to its practice. She was herself very spiritual. Her definition of routine was included in her description of spirituality. Her spiritual faculties of vision and hearing were very well-cultivated and mastered. Through these means her daily life was a routine task. She had a means of traveling from the physical world to any of the others, with the same ease with which one would perform a routine task such as brushing the teeth or taking a bath. In her statement, she was saying that in the practice of spirituality, the same phenomena are experienced again and again; thus, spirituality was a routine task. My mother's words were not clear, to me, then, but I have experienced the phenomena of dreamlike visions routinely since I was five years old and can vouch for her use of the word "routine."

In this earthly life, my mother was clairvoyant and clairaudient. She was the spiritual model who allowed me to experience what others could not see.

This is a book whose story is dedicated to the memory of my mother, Paulina G. Cabezudo, a human life that I loved.

ACKNOWLEDGEMENT

My intention in writing this book is to convey my deepest gratitude to everyone who loved my stories and asked for another book. It is a great privilege to present these warm and spiritually healing stories to everyone who is seeking to be healed.

I am grateful to all the people who made this book a reality. Among these are my parents, for serving as my spiritual models— in particular my mother—for being one of the examples that bestowed upon me a love without any limit. My children: David, whose inner struggle triggered my own spiritual search; Adam, for his silent love and encouragement; and Julie, for her continuously active loving support. I thank my children's families, through their marriages, for their willingness to be nonjudgmental in the areas of nonvisible realms of life. I am also grateful for their sensitivity to concepts and ideas that are different from theirs.

My immediate family, for seeing my light and letting it shine, as well as for all their support, light, and love throughout the years.

Throughout this human experience, I am grateful to my friends, for being what I wanted them to be. In particular to my dear departed friends:

- ❖ Honey Chodan, who was my best friend since high school; until her death from breast cancer, we shared the most important moments in our lives.
- ❖ Diane Yankelovitz, who edited all my research material in health and human services, every book I wrote, and all the conferences

and talks I presented; until her death, we shared the spiritual principles found in this book.

❖ Eric Joubert, another dear friend, who enjoyed reading my conferences and written material; as a clairvoyant and clairsentient himself, he continued to challenge me until the end of his terrestrial journey.

I miss them dearly; may they continue to rest in peace.
Most importantly, I am grateful for The Tingling and the privilege of self-expression with my Soul Spirit.

INTRODUCTION

We can only be said to be alive in those moments when our hearts are conscious of our treasures.

—Thornton Wilder

No man can exist without a maker. In the physical world, we attribute that title to our mother and father. They are the ones we call our parents—our makers. During our early years, it is these people whom we consciously recognize as our first treasures. Then there comes a time when we begin to grow up and start to look deeper into the subject. As you follow the trail in this book that has been prepared for the reader, I hope that you can find some treasures along the way.

This book is my concept of an invisible, formless substance that has become my constant companion. The Tingling is my story— the story of a woman who is in tune with an invisible, formless substance whose idyllic visions are its form of communication. The unique concepts in this book are novel and unexplored areas of healing that have been in my practice for many years. I wanted to share my visions with you in the hope that they would show you a different point of view. I will share with you several meaningful life experiences to best illustrate the methods of communication I maintained with an invisible force I call The Tingling. I hope the framework and patterns of this book enhance your perspective view of the life you are leading. When a human life is searching for enlightenment, an inner invisible force makes the person an inner aspect of the totality. In a sense, understanding this living form and its force is what this book is all about. The conscious awareness of our own evolution in a specific level of understanding is in some factual cases the actual life event, because in the awareness, each is completing the evolutionary phase of that specific event. In this revelation, the individual's level of understanding may differ from one person to another. In fact, understanding one's daily life experience is the key to its force and a person's first step toward enlightenment.

Sometimes, a person has an enlightening discovery and becomes aware of The Tingling in accordance with their level of understanding. The purpose for enlightenment is to activate our soul's evolution. Events are those transitory encounters that we find throughout our daily lives. In fact, I truly believe that life itself is a one-time event of a soul's experience in which each soul has several lifetimes of different phases of being. In any enlightening experience that takes us into another dimension, a person is responding to an event and a force that has the qualities of The Tingling. In this dimension, as we go into separateness, we discover that we have become one. To me, each lifetime seems to be a point in the time-space continuum of a soul, and each point is a life issue that a soul is living. In this belief, the points are lived in order to experience the physical aspect of each issue. The belief also includes a specific number of souls with their multiple points in the same time-space continuum. The points are human lives of a soul in which a person can become aware that each human life has a potential for discovering The Tingling. In addition, the mastery of having a physical experience is a soul's highest goal.

While thinking of writing this book, in my mind's eye I perceived its front cover and the details of each chapter. In my thoughts was a strange feeling, as if the book had already been written. I also sensed that the experiences of another being are contained in this book, along with the strange sensation that the other being and I were one. As my excitement grew stronger, I began to write. In this exhilarating state, I wrote…and I wrote…and I wrote. It was as if I had memorized the words of a book I had already written. I hope it sheds light into your life, as it has done for mine.

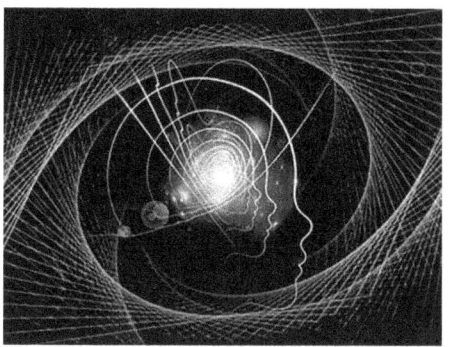

UNION FROM DIVINE ENERGY

How could the drops of water know themselves to be a river? Yet the river flows on.

—Antoine de St. Exupéry

To begin this story, I will have to tell you about the day when I was learning how to meditate. On that day, my world was taken apart in pieces and then returned to its original place. In the process, those things that were dear to me fell apart in front of me, and I was never the same. That day, I was destined to become the new and developed consciousness that followed.

I was fourteen years old when I learned to meditate. The reason I wanted to learn was because I thought it would give me an opportunity to find what was in store for my future. I was under the impression that in a meditative state, I was going to see all the details of the life I was destined to lead. I also felt that knowing my future would allow me to reach my goals in a more precise manner. Along with my future, I wanted to be sure that I was going to be happy for the rest of my life. My need to see the future was due to the confusion I was feeling related to a career and educational path. I felt that by learning to meditate, my destiny would no longer be a mystery to me.

My need to discover what I had come to this world to accomplish was an erroneous thought-form. Within me was a belief system that validated my erroneous thought-forms. Although I was unaware of its existence, the thought-forms of that belief system were controlling my life and the way I behaved toward life. On that day, I discovered that meditation was not going to be a conscious effort for me and that I was already trained to meditate. The day I learned to meditate happened to be a day when everything that I thought was pure and sacred was validated by my own erroneous belief system, a belief system that was ruling the way I behaved toward life. In my belief system, to meditate meant that one was able to leave one's body and travel through space in search of an appropriate life, which in reality was one's future life. In that belief, the erroneous thought-form that surfaced that day was quite interesting.

When I sat to meditate that day, I saw lights bouncing like springs. The lights were bright, and each had its own distinct quality. They resembled miniature stars twinkling upon a background of darkness. The lights appeared to be flashing on and off in a well-organized rhythmic style. It was almost as if they were each performing for a different play on the same stage. After what appeared to be hours, I heard a voice say, "This is it," and all the lights disappeared. The voice was soft, melodic, low as a whisper, and appeared to be coming from a young female. For the next few moments, I saw nothing, and wondered if something needed to be done by me in order to reach my goal. I quickly went through the meditation steps I was given and found I had completed all of them. Then I sat still for several moments longer, and because I was still in the darkness, I deduced that the meditation activity had not yielded the expected results.

While sitting in that "nothingness," I felt that my body was beginning to swirl on its axis. It appeared to be rotating to the right and, at the same time, vibrating in unison with a strong magnetic pull upwards. At this time, I heard a sound that whispered, "You are there," and my eyes opened as if I had awakened from a dream. This voice was identical to the first and sounded almost as if it had been uttered by the same young female.

When I told my mother about my experience, she nodded her head and said, "Good!" After telling several of my friends about the experience, they each said the same thing: "Good!" Wanting to feel "good," I began to formulate definitions for what I had experienced. However, my comprehension level was very limited, and I simply did not understand what was meant by the word "good." A year later, after several similar experiences, I met a woman who explained to me the real purpose of meditation. She said that "in meditation, a person wants to be in 'universality' with their universal prototype." Once again, the explanation was very profound for me. However, this time I knew that any further explanation would be of no use to me, so I simply thanked her.

In the years that followed, I noticed that every time I meditated, it had an overt effect upon my life, and I continued to practice it. Every time I meditated, I felt at peace with myself and with those around me. As the years went by, it became apparent to me that each time I meditated, I felt more conscious of my body and my surroundings. In each meditation, the process I was using was becoming a habit that I deeply enjoyed. My physical life was becoming easier to understand, and my spiritual life appeared to be blending with it. I was beginning to feel at peace with myself at all times, and others were beginning to notice it.

One day, during a meditation, I felt something vibrating around me that I could not see. When I asked in my meditation, "What was that vibration?" the answer was, "It is you!" Because I did not understand the response, according to me, the question had not been answered. My question was specific, and I expected a specific response. I waited silently, hoping that somehow I would receive an answer, but all I heard was the sound of the vibration. Pondering upon the experience, I realized that the vibration was a formless matter that appeared to have the qualities of another form of life. I felt that the vibration was its voice.

The substance I felt around me had mass and weight and a distinct presence that I felt within and around me. Because of its qualities, it had to be alive, but it had to be something other than me. This was the only plausible explanation I had at the time.

As the years went by, I heard many explanations and many profound statements. The thoughts I had created were in some instances flawless; at times, they appeared to answer all my questions, and at other times, they sparked a profound perplexity within me that made me search for more. However, I did not believe that there were life forms besides my own outside of this universe. Hence, I was unable to relate to a formless invisible life that was always within and around me.

Many years later, during my practice of celestial healing, I understood what the lady meant when she said that "in meditation a person wants to be in 'universality' with their universal prototype." At that time, I had begun to practice spiritual healing in my home, and one day, a client told me that he thought I was massaging his stomach deeply and forcefully. The sensation he felt was soothing, strengthening, and healing the pain he was feeling in his stomach. With his eyes closed he said he felt one of my hands inside his stomach. Upon further evaluation, he realized that the hand he felt in his stomach was twice as large as my hand. Then he opened his eyes to see what I was doing and saw that I was sitting in a chair with my eyes close. My hands were resting on my lap and I appeared to be silently praying—my hands were not touching him. When he told me his experience, he said that he had imagined my hand inside his stomach. Since I was unable to give him an explanation for his experience, I remained silent.

This story reappeared several years later, on a Thursday during the month of September. During that time, I was working as a school nurse in a grammar school. I had started a new school year, and my duties as a school nurse had been changed. That year I was going to be more involved with state regulations and the immunization of students with those state mandates. As I prepared to start an immunization clinic, the trail of paperwork became almost unbearable. On that Thursday, I had reached my saturation point and once again became consciously aware of the invisible, formless vibration within and around me.

When I left my office that afternoon, I was mentally drained and physically exhausted. I felt as if the day had been totally wasted with nonsensical activities and was thinking of all the work I still had to do in order to start an immunization clinic at my school site. On my way home, I stopped to visit a friend who was ill and to buy groceries for dinner. During that time I was able to concentrate on something other than the immunization project, and my physical body prepared me for what was yet to come.

When I arrived home, it was seven thirty-five in the evening, and my husband had cooked dinner. The children had already eaten and were working on their school projects for the following day. After changing my clothes, I served myself dinner and noticed that a peaceful vibration was present around and within me. While I ate dinner, the thoughts of the immunization clinic vanished. I knew I was consuming food, but the eating activity felt distant from my mind. During that time, in that physical activity, all I felt was the "nothingness" I often found in my meditations.

While sitting in that "nothingness," I felt that my body was beginning to swirl on its axis. At that point, my eating activity stopped, and my conscious awareness shifted to the "nothingness" around me. It appeared to me that I was rotating to the right and, at the same time, vibrating in unison with a strong magnetic pull upward. I knew then that I was in a meditative state and recognized that in this state, there was peace.

That "nothingness" took me to a place where I was able to hear the sound of music inside my head. As I looked for the source of the sound, the music appeared to come from nowhere. Something was creating a melody that I had heard before, and the instruments were also familiar to me. In the few moments that followed, I heard the music and was able to identify each of the instruments being played and the words as well. The music and its words were sung in the same voice I had heard in the first meditation when I was fourteen years old. When the music stopped, I heard a voice that whispered, "You are there!"

Once again, I was left alone in the dark silver-colored "nothingness" with the peaceful sound of silence. The music had stopped, but the words

"You are there!" continued to linger in my ears. In the "nothingness" I realized that it was in the same voice I had heard singing. Then my eyes opened as if I had awakened from a dream. Assessing my surroundings made me realize that I was sitting at the dinner table and that my food was cold. Although three-fourths of my food remained on my plate, I felt full. My stomach felt as if I had eaten everything in the plate. It had been a long day, and feeling revitalized by an unknown energy, I decided to wash the dishes by hand. In the next few moments while washing the dishes, I wondered how the whole experience was able to take place. Then with the melody in my mind and my eyes open, I continued to hear the words being sung.

Several weeks later, I sat on the piano bench and attempted to reconstruct on the piano what I heard in my head that unforgettable day at the dinner table. To my surprise, the melody and the words were still vivid in my mind. Although I had very little to go by, I was able to play each note on the piano and record the melody and words on a music sheet. I hereby present a musical score fragment of the symbolic image that has remained in my mind.

The memory of that experience and the knowledge gotten as a result are still part of my teaching examples today.

This chapter and its messages are a way to explain how I was able to relate to a formless invisible life that was always within and around me. In this story, I give an example that best illustrates the value of meditation and its reason for allowing one to engage in "universality" with one's universal prototype. By the term prototype, I am referring to that invisible body whose life we are living. It also means that each body lives, regardless of whether we see it or not. Along these lines, the invisible bodies will never interfere or stop the process of anything we choose to do; yet, they are always present and living in their respective dimensions as are the visible ones.

The value of meditation, as presented here, is to allow a "universality" to take place between a meditator and that individual's universal prototype. In this process, the individual's universal prototype has made a union with the person who is meditating. This definition includes the concept that an individual has multiple bodies, visible and invisible, residing in the same point of a time-space continuum.

Included in my definition of "universality" is the union of a being with its primary source.

In our early Western history, shamans were the first to recognize that the human consciousness was part of a larger consciousness. The shaman's tool to reach inner reality is an altered state of consciousness and in their meditations the focus was placed on altered states of consciousness. The philosophers tell us that our soul consciousness lives within, but the methods that are given for realizing it are the pathways of years of isolation. However, the author's research of the literature shows that in our Western culture, consciousness is not understood this way.

Consciousness does not change in any altered state; however, the matter that composes that consciousness is in a space where the molecules form a living body. This space is in the time continuum and is available to every human consciousness. What one senses as an altered state of consciousness is the process of rearranging the molecules. The soul consciousness is the one that will appear to be within. During the time the altered states of consciousness are in progress, the individual will experience his own level of awareness and his one-time event will continue to thrive.

To answer the questions whether consciousness has levels and if there is a higher consciousness, one has to recognize that consciousness itself is in levels of awareness and that levels of awareness are part of our concept of linear growth. In reality, there is only one consciousness which is experienced by each individual's level of awareness. It is this consciousness that people call a higher consciousness; a term used by those whose personal perception is that of a lower being.

As the mind separates from the physical body, it can concentrate on another body. In order for this to occur, the mind must be in the same point of a time-space continuum in which another body resides. The same is true when we meditate. A union in meditation occurs when one is perfectly aligned with all the multiple bodies in a point of a time-space continuum. When the bodies align themselves in a point of a time-space continuum and the mind separates, the inevitable result is "universality." In addition, to further understand this concept, it is of tremendous advantage to have experienced the different levels of states of consciousness through the art of meditation.

I realized that I and a formless, invisible being were one, as I relived that point in my time-space continuum. The Tingling is a concept of "universality" in which there is a very close relationship with an invisible, formless macro sphere. The belief of this phenomenon, along with some examples, is found in the explanations I give in this book. In retrospect, I have experienced this phenomenon many times, and it appears to be in the lives of others as well. It has the qualities of another being watching over me while I experience its life. In fact, it became the source of healing I practice. In other words, I have a conscious union with The Tingling as it heals the lives I come in contact with. That "universality" was the primary reason for conducting the research studies that led me to write this book.

LAW OF GROUP CONSCIOUSNESS

All truths are easy to understand once they are discovered; the point is to discover them.

—Galileo Galilei

During the several years that followed, I have been meditating in the same manner as I did when I was fourteen years old. The time of day was always the same and in the same place: in my home on Thursdays. The purpose of this ritual is to unite with like minds and conduct my own celestial healing service as an invisible helper, and thus contribute to the well-being of our universe. The meditations were always implemented in the same manner; however, on one particular Thursday prior to my meditation, I thought of a very interesting format. As I prepared myself to meditate on that Thursday, I decided to implement the new format; it was a meditation that turned out to be the most glorious experience of my life.

On this particular Thursday, instead of meditating in the silvery "nothingness" to which I had been accustomed, I thought of starting the meditation by mentally creating a room by the seashore. My original intention was to release any tension I had acquired during the day. In my usual meditation space, I started to imagine that I was in a room by the seashore and that my tension was drifting among the warm waves of the ocean stream. As my body started to relax, I had a vision of myself in which I had the form of a bell. I was trying to create a thought-form of a small room by the seashore, which I did, and at the same time created a beautiful relationship with the consciousness of a bell.

When I think of that continuous point in space, as well as the experiences of that Thursday, I can sense the bell and see how it became alive. The small room by the seashore was exactly what I wanted to create in my mind that day. It was a perfect replica! All my undertakings and desires were supplanted in this room. Every cell in my body told that I was in the right divine place. In this respect, my thought-form was perfect and complete. To say the least, creating a small room by the seashore had been a success.

Once I had created the room in my mind, I looked around for the best place to start a meditation. In the center of the room was a wooden rocking chair, carefully placed on top of a white crocheted rug. Directly in front of the rocking chair was a wide panoramic picture window without curtains or glass. To the left side of the window wall was a large shiny bronze bell. When I focused on it, I felt something strange. The bell felt alive whenever I was attuned to the mind of the bell. The window appeared to be the main entrance to the room. Since there was only one place to sit, I sat on the wooden rocking chair and began to meditate. While sitting on the wooden rocking chair from my vantage point, I began to explore my surroundings. Directly in front of me I could see the seashore. It was late in the evening, and the weather appeared to be warm. From inside the room, I could feel the moisture of the sea. As I listened closely, I noticed that the strong tide of the peaceful seashore could be heard inside the room. The sound of the sea echoed in the room, creating a perfect meditation chant. I could also hear the water splashing against a rock in front of the little room by the seashore. I had a sense I was going to enjoy meditating in this room.

As I began to feel the sound of silence within myself, I also felt a profound sense of peace. Amidst this profound peace in the small room by the seashore, I felt the consciousness of the bell. In what appeared to be a deep meditation, I felt as if I were inside the bell. Along the curvature of the bell, I felt the moist coolness of the late evening air. This experience was my first, and I felt that the bell felt the same. On that day, my mind and the bell's mind became engaged in a divine conversation. I felt certain that in our dialogue that Thursday was an agreement whose memory will remain with me throughout the years. During the time I remained in the consciousness of the bell, I do not recall losing the path or the inability to concentrate on my own consciousness. The most striking difference was its willingness to share its space and the tremendous amount of collaboration it furnished to the consciousness of the bell. It felt as though it was an observer and a commentator for the interpretation of the various symbolic images that were presented in the vision. Yet, I was also aware that the consciousness of the bell was sharing and occupying its space.

While in this state, something alerted me that there was a message for me in the bell experience. In the message was the assurance that the decision to be healed was mine. With great wonderment at the time, I asked myself if a body that is in the physical plane could respond to a celestial healing in another plane. My immediate response was an emphatic "Yes!" In other words, this meant that those clients who were being healed by our invisible helpers were receiving the celestial healing in another spiritual plane. I believe that along with showing me that an aspect of myself needed to be healed, the bell experience also caused me to question the psychic change I felt within me. The experience sparked a resonant chord within me. For some strange reason, I sensed that it was important to understand the relationship between the bell and myself. In the bell was a resonant chord that told me when I had entered the plane I occupied. Its glorious chime was the voice of the bell.

Besides uniting and becoming one with the bell, I was able to be in complete alignment with the invisible amorphous mind of the bell. Then when the bell was no longer a part of my conscious awareness the meditation ended as if the bell had actually lived. After that first meditation in the small room by the seashore, I had the following questions:

- ❖ Where was my consciousness during the time I was the bell?
- ❖ Why was the bell by the window?
- ❖ When was this bell formed in my mind?
- ❖ Does the matter of the bell have the same qualities and dimensions of living matter?
- ❖ What was the rationale for knowing that the bell was alive?

The answers to these questions will be written in this chapter, along with the life I was leading. They also address the erroneous belief I had in discordance with the theory of the law of truth. In this law, truth is defined as highest wisdom or the complete answer to any given issue. This definition takes into account:

- the truths which are found in our biocomputer,
- our thought-forms,
- an individual's entire system of beliefs,
- our levels of consciousness, and
- our symbolic images.

What I propose for the first question—Where was my consciousness during the time I was the bell?—may be difficult to understand. I will present it here for your careful speculation in order that the question can be answered. My proposition is based on the theory that every erroneous belief has a corresponding erroneous truth. When the question is understood according to the theory of the law of truth, the experience of the bell makes a more penetrating, delicate—and perhaps subtle—sense. Therefore, to answer the question "Where was my consciousness during the time I was the bell?" I can say that I strongly sensed when the awareness of my consciousness was focused upon the living qualities of the bell. In my point in space, the bell and I united.

During this meditative space, the bell tolled when I was in complete alignment with the invisible formless mind of the bell. I also noticed that whenever I was consciously aware of my mind, I was able to see the bell. The bell and I were sharing that point in space. During those short moments, the bell and I were enclosed in one consciousness.

The question "Why was the bell by the window?" has many answers, all of which I feel are valid. To maintain the trend of thought flowing, I will choose an answer that explains how I was misusing the law of truth. I will submit one that I feel is the stem to the law of truth. According to the law of truth, every erroneous belief has a corresponding truth. In my case, the corresponding truth was that all matter is alive; with that thought in mind, let us answer the question "Why was the bell by the window?" In the room I had created in my mind that Thursday, the panoramic window represented the only entrance to another level of my conscious mind. It was the only entrance to the nurturing chamber of my inner levels of truth. If all matter is alive, then in the meditative chamber everything was alive.

We can also say that by the window was the most logical spot for the bell. Well, it was there where, after entering the small room by the seashore, one entered into the interior levels of my truth and where the coalition of our minds took place. By including the bell inside the room, it is to be understood that this is an aspect of yourself that needs to be healed. That level of my conscious mind was saying that in the life I was leading I was misusing one of nature's laws. This answer stems from the theory of the law of truth. It is included here in the hope that it will shed light upon your own life, as well as upon your erroneous beliefs.

In the answer to the next question—When was this bell formed in my mind?—is another part of the theory to the law of truth. If I were creating a bell in my mind, the specifics of that detail would be clear. The little room by the seashore I was trying to create was in essence a place to be alone with the consciousness of a higher being. Its design was what I considered essential to a good meditation. A bell would be one of those things that I would have to eliminate, since it would have no obvious function in that room. In a sense, the bell would serve only as an inanimate decoration for the room. Because the bell had no use to me in the meditation chamber, I believe the bell was not formed by me in my mind.

If the above is true, then by whom or where was the bell formed? I believe the idea of a bell was already in that level of my conscious mind. This belief is easily explained with the theory of the law of truth. In the bell was a consciousness that I perceived as having thoughts and beliefs that differ from mine. Within the depth of my being, something alerted me to remain a short while with the bell. Every time I was completely aligned with the consciousness of the bell, the bell tolled three times. Then, in the consciousness of the bell I could see the psychic myths of my own consciousness. In fact, in the consciousness of the bell, I could perceive that my own matter was distinctly separate from the bell. In the level of consciousness I have, the question "Does the matter of the bell have the same qualities and dimensions of living matter?" is not easily explained. The way I answer this question is to ask another one: "What are the qualities and dimensions of living matter?" This question can be answered in two ways.

- First, I can describe each quality and each dimension of living matter and compare each to those of the bell. However, if I answer by comparing each of the qualities and dimensions of living matter, the matter of the bell will not be included.
- A second way to answer this question is to describe the overall appearance of living matter. If I answer by describing the overall appearance of living matter, then the matter of the bell will be included.

I will add here that to respond to this question in this manner won't be simple. I think that, for each human being, the process of formulation of ideas cannot rise above the things he knows; hence, this question is not simple to answer. Thus, I will leave it to you, the reader, and your formulation of advanced ideas.

The last question—What was the rationale for knowing that the bell was alive?—may be a key to the formulation of your own ideas. The answer to this question depends on whether you sense that all matter is alive. For me, the answer to this question is the most winsome formulation of ideas in my mind. In my belief was an erroneous thought that played a role in what I accepted as truth. This experience demonstrated to me that the bell's matter and mine were alike. Since I believed that I was alive, the experience of being one with the bell was the proof to believe that the matter of the bell was also alive. For me, the answer to this question supplied the corresponding truth to my erroneous belief, as well as healed a wounded aspect of myself. The corresponding truth was that the type of matter found in the bell was the same type of matter I had, and since I am an animate matter, the bell also is. In the belief system I had were two categories of matter: animate and inanimate. In this belief, each category of matter was in a class of its own. I felt that I had an animate conscious mind and inanimate objects did not. I also felt unable to understand that it was possible to transfer thoughts to or from the two categories.

Last, I felt that because I could not communicate with an inanimate matter, it was incapable of thinking and hence had no living attribute. In this belief, I was not unique. The thought-forms responsible for my belief were taught to me in grammar school. We learn to separate matter in this manner early in life. It is understood by everyone that inanimate objects are things that are seen but do not have life. In school, we study the molecular structure of inanimate things, but we are not taught any programs to communicate with them. In accordance with the understanding that has been given to us, we formalize the basis for our behavior toward inanimate objects and respond accordingly. This experience proved to me that there is only one category of matter, and that all matter lives and breathes like I do.

The law of truth basically says that complete truth is operating and present at all times, in every given situation. To understand this law in its totality, we must be aware of the levels of consciousness that are possible in an individual. The individual who perceives his own level of consciousness can also experience his own truth.

In our human consciousness is a built-in biocomputer that programs every space in time. In the bank of symbolic images found within it are the elements of our thought-forms. To the biocomputer, a human thought-form has to conform to beliefs that are upheld as truths. In this theory, the biocomputer functions according to our level of consciousness and our belief system. When our truth is based on a point of view, the validity of the thought-forms in our biocomputer will also be based on that point of reference.

Hence, the truth of that point of view and all that is based on it will always be worthy of truth for that individual. That being so in any given level of consciousness, our thought-forms are validated by those truths found in our biocomputer. The only thing misleading us, which can perhaps lead us astray, is the way those thought-forms take us to a point at which the erroneous thoughts are validated by our erroneous truths.

Another aspect of importance is the principle or the pathway one is leading in life. This principle and its theory will be briefly discussed here because it has many complex related thoughts within itself. For this discussion, it is important to know that a principle in life can be defined as a group of thought-forms that propels an individual into an unexplainable course of action. These thought-forms contain the entire mission of one's life. In this mission are the symbolic images and the truths that are to be achieved by them. They also serve as a guide for an individual's belief system and the ideas s/he accepts as truth.

In my spiritual healing practice, I have found that when my clients' bodies are not in alignment with their principle in life, the result is always a feeling of being "out of tune" with their lives. In this feeling of discontent, the client becomes the victim of a closed system that refuses to open itself to new possibilities. At the same time, their self-validating feedback loop becomes a reason for their feelings of discontent. I have also found that once the principle of the client's life is discovered and understood, the life of the individual takes on a different radiance, and in so doing, s/he becomes a conscious traveler along a carefully chosen path.

In my search, I discovered that each client's pathway was responsible for every so-called accident and/or serendipitous incident in their lives. From this, I deduce that one's pathway in life is the core and purpose for living. This is the aspect of my theory that has been the most difficult for my clients to grasp, yet it has been the most tangible in my own life.

Embedded in this theory is the concept that belief systems have a direct influence on the way one experiences the universe. One's belief system is formulated by the many ideas one entertains throughout the formative years. The most convincing ideas will remain to serve as validation for our belief system and, obviously, end up being a part of our truths. During the course of one's life, the validated truths become the individual's belief system. Whether these truths are correct or not, it is our nature to respond to physical and psychological symptoms based on the validity they have at the time.

In my own belief system, the universe and the perceptions one has of it are experienced through the senses of the individual body's mechanism. A good example of this is illness and the "sick role" played by each individual. When the individual believes that s/he is sick, the response is to accept the perceptions of illness along with its corresponding "sick role." The belief in illness basically says that the physical body is capable of becoming sick. This belief incorporates a way to respond to the specific type of illness and the type of behavior for the "sick role" that is being played.

I also think that because the individual believes in illness, all disharmonious events are held in some part of the physical body as they occur. Thus, for every part of the physical body, there must be a series of symbolic images to explain each illness. At the same time, these will influence the individual in the belief in illness as well as in the "sick role" that will be played. In short, I believe that all this is an offer, seemingly without commitment, that influences the individual directly on how s/he can experience the universe. So, in essence, our belief systems are based on whatever the individual has formulated for himself.

In this universe, our laws of life are many; some are explained in this book. Among these laws we find the underlying truths for our forms of life. They lead us to a level of understanding where our lives have a definite purpose and a definite meaning for every being in this universe. It's almost as though the laws are fundamental to every life form. They lay the foundation that is to become our earthly system of beliefs as well as our psychic myths. Through our laws of life a person's beliefs have an effect upon their physical world and determine their state of psychological and/or physical well being.

Experiencing the laws of life and their invisible thoughts is the primary focal place for our journey. When the nature of a law is understood in the life we lead, our consciousness changes and in so doing, so does our belief system. In addition, the person's psychological and/or physical state of well being also changes. In the daily events of our normal everyday life, we find the arena to interpret each law. Because these laws are understood by the individual at his level of consciousness, in his understanding there is a change in how he responds to life.

According to the capacity of each individual, those laws that are of a spiritual nature have as their basis a method to validate the things we know, and as our conscious awareness is developed, so is our level of understanding. Each law corresponds to the spiritual nature or the order of importance of our Soul Spirit and is at our disposal as often as needed during our normal daily living. The laws of life that are found in this book are those which this author personally experienced and understands. The spiritual laws found in this book are examples of the key roles they played in my life. The invisible living form showed me how to understand these fundamental laws in the life I was leading and ultimately becoming my spiritual source of strength.

It is believed that mystics possess knowledge known only to their cult. This belief portrays other individuals as human beings without the caliber of the inner force of the mystic. In this belief, a mystic who possesses all knowledge can be the only one with the inner force. This belief is in opposition to a fundamental law which does not discriminate between human beings. It is a force within each and every one of us—a universal divine force that belongs to all of us.

There are other beliefs that operate within us in a similar manner. One of these is the belief in levels of diseases. It can portray itself in:

the belief that a food allergy can turn into a cancerous esophagus, a belief that some people can be healthier than others, and the belief that an emotional disease can lead to a stomach ulcer.

The three beliefs mentioned above are in opposition to a law and can be changed. This is true for any psychic myth we may encounter throughout our lives. When our erroneous thoughts are validated by our erroneous truths, our belief system is also erroneous. This is one of the reasons why people behave the way they do. The individual that is validating his erroneous thoughts is always under the impression that the other person is wrong. I believe that most people are genuinely caring toward others. In their minds, they feel they have been modest, honest, reasonable, and affectionate. They often feel their behavior is correct and see no reason to change.

Once their erroneous beliefs are understood and they change, the person becomes another person, and we begin to see all the qualities they profess to have. In essence, if you want to change the disharmony in the life you are leading, you must first see how you have set in motion the person, the situation, and/or the condition. When the self becomes aware of its personality and responds to a wounded aspect of itself, the awareness, I believe, can change the self; however, the mere awareness is simply a reminder that all our bodies are not in perfect harmony. The change is accomplished when the bodies are place in perfect alignment with each other. This belief defines the personality as the entity that resides inside the self. In the mind of the person responding to the awareness, there is a conscious understanding that results in a behavioral change that other people can see. The mind awareness is the same and causes the same change in each one of us. However, the interpretation of the awareness differs according to our level of understanding and the life we are leading. The interpretation is never wrong when we are conscious of our life's events, and at the end of our journey, by remembering the experience, the person is blessed.

In any uplifting of humanity, there is a subterfuge based on defined thought-forms. Along with this, there is also a shift in consciousness that sparks the individual into self-analysis. The starting point to study our experiences is that shift in consciousness. As we proceed in this self-analysis, every contact we make with another person will become another confirmation of the experience. Any experience that challenges our conscious awareness can literally cause a change in our behavior. The change in behavior will have a concurrent physical change in the person. When this occurs, I believe our principles are stimulated by the experience, and simultaneously, we and our lives will also be part of any change. If the experience is unique, there will be a definite response related to it. When the response goes above what we consciously know or beyond our belief system, it will in turn bring about a challenge shift according to the motion of our expectations. In such case, when the ingratiating experience responds according to our ideas, the personality has been healed. Because this is true, that physical body, in its corresponding plane of existence, will also be healed.

One of the best examples that can be given here is the experience of hating another person. To study this experience, we must first have a shift in consciousness related to our fundamental beliefs. In this example, it is the person we hate that sparks the tremulous feeling of hatred within us. If we respond to the spark of hatred by ignoring the person, other opportunities will come to us; other people will come into our lives to confirm the experience. On the other hand, if we confront the spark of that tremulous hatred and conduct a self-analysis, that experience will produce a change in our consciousness. To understand the hatred, in the subsequent case, one must first feel hatred, and in that awareness, one will have a concurrent physical change. The change that occurs in our behavior (personality) begins in our minds.

As we love the behavioral change, we begin to feel less self-hatred and also begin to love the person we hated. When we feel loved by others, the behavioral change will be confirmed by the people who come into our lives. The change is also evident in our lives through the new perspective we demonstrate toward the person we hated. To understand that this hate may exist within us is to uplift ourselves. The individual who follows this process is always changing his personality and, in this manner, healing those aspects that appear to cause aversion toward other people: those aspects of himself that he dislikes in other people.

When we change the way we think in this manner, a dark cloud is removed, and like magic, a light is turned on. The new change has an effect on our lives, and we become the product of that change. In the bell experience, the "me" I knew became one with the consciousness of the bell. The feeling led me to a sense of formless awareness and to an inner world of a bell. In this invisible form, something inside of me was showing me what it felt to be a bell. It was showing me that the bell had feelings of its own.

The experience I had with the bell was related to the law of group consciousness and the law of truth. In my erroneous belief, I was living in opposition to these laws. The bell experience was a way for me to understand how I was misusing each law. In my mind, all the life forms of matter were different and that erroneous belief was related to an erroneous truth. In order to master the pathway I was working under, I also had to master the law of truth.

In this meditation, I discovered a different way of entering into an altered state of consciousness. The experience of being something inanimate and other than "me" was strange but humbling. After I had entered the imaginary small room by the seashore and had aligned with the consciousness of the bell, the bell tolled three times. I learned, in the form of a bell, that everything is alive. I believed that human beings could not communicate with inanimate objects, and this experience showed me that my belief was wrong. In the body of the bell, the "me" I knew felt as if it was having a "bell experience," but in reality, I was experiencing a vision and at the same time traveling in the invisible form of a bell.

In the bell experience, an erroneous thought was changed in my mind, and in doing so, I was given the opportunity to heal those aspects of myself that were not in accordance with the law of truth. This has been one of the ways for me to bring those erroneous thought-forms to the surface. Among these exhilarating experiences are the inner thoughts I hold as my truths, and now they are part of my new belief system.

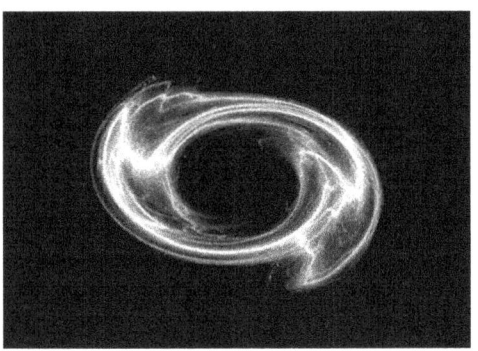

THE STRANGER, A VOICE, THAT PROCESS

Nothing said to us, nothing we can learn from others, reaches us so deep as that which we find in ourselves.

—Theodore Reik

In this particular story, I am living with my husband and children in the state of California. As my present life unfolds before me, I am traveling to work. In this journey, I am traveling by car and find myself in the car with an invisible stranger. This is a stranger whose voice I perceived through dreamlike visions. The story I have selected for this chapter is about that invisible stranger, the voice I perceived and that process.

My journey begins on a glorious and memorable Thursday in the middle of the month of May. Waking up early in the morning when I lifted my head up from the pillow that Thursday felt good to me. Then I turned my head toward my bedroom window and immediately confirmed that for me it was going to be a good day. From my vantage point, I could see that the day was clear and the leaves on the trees still had their morning dew. Within my bedroom, I could smell the fresh, crisp morning air. It felt like one of those days when one is glad to be alive. I had scheduled many routine tasks for that day and as most people do. I wondered what other tasks this day had to offer. That glorious morning, I had a strong, heartfelt sensation that something wonderful was about to take place, because there was an aura of glee throughout the air.

Before I could give myself an answer to what the day had to offer, I left my bed as usual and prepared myself for work. I was working in a metropolitan area, in a grammar school with 1,690 students, as a school nurse. Included in my school nursing duties were conducting health workshops for students in kindergarten through sixth grade. I taught them classes in dental hygiene, basic first aid, drug abuse, sex education, and other topics that teachers felt were related to health issues. That day, I had scheduled a workshop for teachers on cardiopulmonary resuscitation for their continuing education credits. This day was the beginning of their testing practice and their written test. Since the teachers were very interested in this course, I was also excited about the class.

During the period of time I served as a school nurse in this school, the work I had done was taken very seriously by the teachers, students, and staff. Perhaps it was my love for nursing, or their love for teaching, or that I was the only medical person in this school. Whatever the reasons, I felt that my work and teachings were taken very seriously, and the school personnel were all very supportive of me.

I left my bed and began to prepare myself for work in my customary manner. As usual, I left my home at six in the morning for work. On my way to work I perceived that there was "something" around me. I turned off the music that was playing from my car radio, and attempted to give my undivided attention to what I perceived. The sense that there was something surrounding me became stronger, yet there was no visible evidence to explain its presence.
In my immediate surrounding I felt a strong presence and a strong sound of silence. Along the way, the presence felt heavy, as if it had substance; however, I was the only visible being in my car. Halfway to my destination, the traffic slowed down, and I found myself at a complete stop, waiting for the railroad train to pass.

While I waited for the train to pass, I had a dreamlike vision in which I saw myself as a child. In the vision, I saw myself as a young child, about four years of age, in a house of familiar scent. My memory drifted to my childhood and all the years I spent in that house. In the vision, the house appeared exactly like the one in which I had spent most of my younger years. My life as a child also appeared to be the same. The vision felt as if I were returning to the memory of that childhood. It felt as though the appearance of that house brought with it a memory that was still vivid in my mind. From inside the house, the child could see through the window and saw that it was raining outside. Surrounding the child's body was an invisible living form, and I felt its presence. Hence, as a child I had also felt its presence. At times, I felt the child's thoughts and sensed her frustration of wanting her mother and not being able to be with her. As the child, I was looking at myself in a mirror, as if there were someone on the other side of the mirror. In the same room was a woman who was deeply engrossed in reading a letter and I felt as if I were alone in the house. In my mind, as an adult, the thoughts appeared to be real because the vision allowed me to see an event from my past.

As a young child, I saw myself acting out a dreamlike vision through a myth. In that dreamlike vision, it felt like I was recalling my actual dreams. I sensed that every day I looked for things to materialize in my environment like the ones that appeared to me in my dreams. I also sensed that as a child the dreams I had at night were always prophetic in nature and that I found myself believing in them. When the dreamlike vision appeared to me this time, instead of looking at the details as the adult that I was, I responded as the child had then, and thought it was all in my mind.

The details I saw in the dreamlike vision represented those events in my mind that I felt strongly about. They had the characteristics of wanting to heal others. I noticed that in the details of every dreamlike vision, the message was the same. Each dreamlike vision predicted what I hoped would take place and added a new symbolic detail, but I saw that the same format and presence was surrounding me in every dreamlike vision.

When I understood those reasons, the dreamlike visions stopped; I was then approximately six or seven years old.

As I waited for the railroad train to pass, the thoughts of me as a child were very lucid, as if I were reliving the past. I sensed that embedded in the memory I had recalled was the explanation for what I perceived around me. During the time it took for the railroad train to pass, my concept of time had stopped. Throughout this time, I was also oblivious of my surrounding panoramic view. In these few minutes, I had relived several childhood years and saw myself acting out a myth. The vision had enlightened me in these few minutes, and given me an idea.

In the memory of something that happened many years ago an answer to a belief system emerged. It occurred to me that the answer to what I perceived around me was in the memory of my past as a child. In this experience, I learned that what I perceived to be around me was with me when I was four years old or perhaps from the beginning of my own existence. The idea of something having the power to separate yet be present had an element of intrigue for me. This dreamlike vision, and its point in space, was also very dynamic in scope. The invisible form I perceived around me and within me had to be related to the memory I held of myself as a child.

My thoughts went back to myself as the child who seemed to be convinced that an invisible form was living within her. She accepted its presence as herself, and to her, that presence was all. In fact, the life she was leading with the invisible form was similar to the thoughts in her mind. The house and the experiences she had in it were stored in the memories of the four-year-old. In her experiences, the child appeared to have mastered a part of her that was formless. At the end of the dreamlike vision, I returned to the awareness of sitting in a car waiting for the railroad train to pass, with a perceived idea that there was something around me. The vision took me along a strange journey. As I traveled its path, it became crystal clear to me that in my car was an invisible form whose presence I had felt and accepted at four years of age.

When I arrived to work that day, the perception I had of something being around me felt real. It had the qualities of having consciousness and seemed to be alive. As I entered the main office, it appeared to follow me in close proximity in a mass of solid yet formless matter. I also paid close attention to the presence and noticed its tranquilizing vibrations and its peaceful sound. The presence accompanied me into my office and remained with me throughout the day.

I cannot recall what happened after I walked into my office. After the above experience, the day seemed to have passed quickly. However, I am very clear about the presence around me that day. It has left a mark that I chose to use as a midpoint in my life. Now I refer to this point as the line of demarcation between before and after the presence.

To me, this dreamlike vision had many logical questions that had to be answered. While searching for the answers in my mind to other experiences, the following questions came into my mind:

- ❖ Where did the formless, invisible vibration come from?
- ❖ When did the formless, invisible vibration come into my life?
- ❖ When does the formless, invisible vibration come to me?
- ❖ What does the formless, invisible vibration want from me?

The first question—Where did the formless, invisible vibration come from?—is still being researched. In order to follow a specific trend of thought, this question has to be answered in the past level of consciousness and in a simplistic fashion. In my past level of consciousness, I thought that the world was experienced through the physical body. To make some sense of the life I was leading, I operated on the premise that the physical body was a tool for experiencing the outer world. In this belief, I was in a physical body to live certain experiences handed down by an unknown source that had my best interest at heart. With this level of consciousness, I believe the invisible presence came to me from that belief of an unknown source. The way I answered the question—Where did the formless, invisible vibration come from?—at that time did not explain why the unknown source had decided to send a formless vibration that I was unqualified and inadequately prepared to receive. Because that answer further failed to explain where the unknown source came from, to me, it was the primary reason for rejecting it.

The second question—When did the formless, invisible vibration come into my life?—is much easier to answer and easier to explain. In the vision, I was taken to a house of familiar scent. The house was where I lived from one-year-old until I was six and a half years old. It is my belief that the vision was a way for me to recall the memory of the time I was four years old. As an adult, I had forgotten that the presence was always with me, and in recalling that memory, I also recalled when the presence was with me. The vision specifically showed me the time when I was four years old. It stands to reason that it had come into my life during that time, between one year old and four, or perhaps my life and its life began at the same time. However, the dreamlike vision was very specific: It was showing me the time in my life when I had felt and accepted its presence. That brings us to the next question: "When does the formless, invisible vibration come to me?" This question can be answered in two ways: (1) by my past level of consciousness, or (2) by my present level of consciousness. When answering with my past level of consciousness, the concept of an unknown source is used. In the vision, I saw myself at times that were critical in my life. During all those times, the presence of the formless vibration was visible to me. This means that the unknown source is all- knowing and sends the formless, invisible vibration when there is disharmony around me. When answering with my present level of consciousness, moving the trend of thought along the lines of prophetic thoughts will also give us an answer. When I use the principle of prophetic thoughts, I am deducing that the formless, invisible vibration comes to me before a problem occurs. At that time, it shows me what I need to know and what I can do ahead of time. In so doing, it allows me to prepare myself for whatever role I am to play. This also means that the formless, invisible vibration shows me only the portion of the given event that applies to my personal involvement and action. Dreamlike visions are moving thought-forms that tell a story. The story is always connected to the individual who is experiencing the dreamlike vision. While experiencing this type of vision, the individual is in suspended animation and time as we know it stops. The only thing that remains constant is the conscious mind. Dreamlike visions are useful when there are questions within us to be answered, because the meanings to the experiences we are unable to explain are presented in our moving thoughts. It is a way to have a first-hand experience of seeing the answers to our lives. When we experience and tour each day beforehand, the life we are leading is opened for us, and at the end of the tour, our lives are healed.

Each dreamlike vision represents an aspect of the life we are leading. Within each moving thought is a symbolic interpretation that answers a given belief and our lives begin to make some sort of sense. When our conscious mind is absorbed in a dreamlike vision, the life we are leading becomes meaningful. In fact, a dreamlike vision may have an explanation for the way we perceive life that may change our lives.

In a dreamlike vision, the thought-forms are alive, and because the thoughts are alive, their energy is allowed to travel. Along the journey, the living thoughts come in contact with other living vibrations, and throughout the journey, they will unite with those of similar vibrations. As they unite with others, their energy strengthens and, in doing so, materializes. The same is true of the thought-forms that are stored in our human biocomputer.

The way in which we act out the daily life we lead is through a memory of our dreams. Our lives have been a series of points in a time-space continuum. In our daily events, as we live our daily lives, the manuscript that we act out is written from the memory of those points in space where we have lived. To understand a dreamlike vision, we must first understand the meaning of its symbols. In their definition, we will find the specific association one has for the symbol itself. Once this is found, it is important to be paying close attention to whether it applies to healing oneself or to those people or situations you are assisting to heal.

The fourth question, "What does the formless, invisible vibration want from me?" has to be answered in my present level of consciousness. When I look back at the times I have been with the formless, invisible vibration, the following answer to this question makes more sense to me. In my answer is embedded a belief that needs to be briefly explained. It relates to why we attune to higher vibrations, and how each person is seeing the same thing from several different points of vision. In this question, the following points can be made:

- The formless vibration is visible to me; therefore, it wants the point of vision to be placed on me.
- Through me, it has a visible form of life in which it can express itself to others; therefore, it wants to work with me.
- It also wants the healing ability to flow through me; in so doing, it also heals me.
- It is teaching me to become a spiritual healer and thus heal others; therefore, it wants me to teach others what it's teaching me.

In this vision, there were a series of questions pertaining to the vision that I vowed would be answered. In these questions were the answers to my life and a way to become healed. They pertained to the need within me to know

- ❖ why the invisible form was in my car,
- ❖ why the vision was of my past, and
- ❖ why it had chosen the time when I was four years old.

As I began to answer these questions, I realized that my level of consciousness was changing and inside of me was a new point of vision that sparked a desire to learn more about the formless invisible vibration. As I felt more comfortable with my first visions, I experienced others. When I understood the answers to the pertinent questions of each vision, I had other visions. The subsequent visions and their explanations became easier to understand once I became familiar with their symbols. With the passing of time, I grew in many ways, and I looked forward to the visions and developed a tremendous gratitude toward the presence of the invisible form.

When our relationship became closer, the focus of the visions also became more intimate, and their intention was to explain a law. It was almost as if I were becoming more comfortable with discussions of personal matters and of an intimate nature. The invisible form and I continued to communicate with each other throughout the years in the same manner, with the exception that the visions were different in content and different in what they were intending to explain in my life. My life experiences were giving me the answers contained in the visions. During those years, my life became an arena in which to experience the visions. By pondering upon the experiences and detaching from the outcome, the explanations were attainable. There were subtle changes in my life, such as: changes in the relationship among my immediate family, and changes in my perception of how I viewed my relationship with them.

Describing the visions seems to be the best way of relating my story. Therefore, I wrote the experiences that I thought would be most appropriate when describing the communication process and its way of explaining a fundamental law. This vision and its journey by inner projection was the means used by an invisible formless vibration to communicate with me. I perceived its form with all my senses as it spoke to me via visions. I present this story to show how the life I led was explained to me by an invisible presence, as well as how through the interpretation of a relationship with an invisible presence that communicated with me through conscious visions, the invisible presence began to pave the way of the life I was leading. This vision made me aware that we have several spiritual bodies.

This story is an example of how The Tingling communicated with me through inner projection. In this method, the conscious awareness is transferred from the physical or surface mind bodies to an inner body in order that the inner body may then travel to another location or stay in the same location as the physical body, while having experiences on another level of vibration. Let me pause here for a moment to differentiate between projecting in the astral body and projecting in an inner body. An inner body projection is not another name for an astral projection. In an inner projection, we leave the physical body under the guidance of

The Tingling and travel in either the etheric body or in an astral body, which is commonly referred to as the feeling body. The departure and arrival to the physical body is accomplished without being aware of a connecting cord or without seeing the physical body as unoccupied.

The dreamlike vision in this chapter not only taught me, but explained my erroneous belief system as well. I have a strong feeling that the vision had a purpose and that every event stemming from it allowed my soul to evolve. The sensation of release that the explanations brought to my conscious awareness were answers to the myths I was living. These explanations were giving me an understanding of the myths, as well as their corresponding truths. While I attempted to correct the myths that I was following, it became apparent to me that the awareness allowed me to trust my feelings; although no one appeared to notice, with each vision my present life had a deeper meaning and my life had begun to change.

The stories in this book consist of these types of phenomena, which make the dreamlike visions come alive. The person who relates to life in this manner is consciously evolving, truly gifted, and in tune with The Tingling. When the formless vibration is visible to others in the same way it is to me, this explanation will be understood and the system of health care in this country will be in sync with all those celestial healers that are walking along a similar pathway with me.

THE TINGLING FAMILY

Nothing is so strong as gentleness, nothing so gentle as real strength.

—St. Francis de Sales

My journey continued on a Thursday when all my children and my husband were in bed. It was approximately midnight when I returned to my bedroom. Looking at the sky through my living room window, I could see that the sun had retired, leaving its reflection to the moon. Although the moon was out of sight, I could see that it had taken its place in the sky. The reflection of the moon illuminated every point in my visual space. I begin my story on that glorious and satisfying Thursday.

Looking at the sky through my living room window, I started to recall the events of that day. My day began with going to work as usual and meeting the tasks of a school nurse. According to those involved, I had resolved many issues and everyone was obviously satisfied with the results of my tasks. So I planned the tasks for the following day and confirmed the plan with the office staff, to make sure we all had the same plan, and left the office knowing that it had been an eventful day.

Upon arriving at my home Andrew [my son] was waiting for me. He had injured his arm in an after-school football practice. I looked at his injuries and decided to take him to an after-hours physician. I found a doctor who was on call at the Naval Hospital and decided to call him. When the nurse answered the telephone and heard my case, she told me to bring my son and have the doctor on call examine the injury. I left a message for my husband with my daughter and proceeded with my son to the Naval Hospital. Dr. Mack [the doctor on call], awakened from his sleep, examined my son and, in almost a textbook manner, performed his assessment of my son's injury. The visit revealed a broken thumb, which required a short arm cast and a long visit to the doctor. When we returned home, Jarrod [my other son] was waiting for us. He had aggravated an old injury to his hand in an after-school activity. I observed his injuries and decided to take him to the same after-hours physician. Dr. Mack, awakened from his sleep once again, examined Jarrod and, once again, in almost a textbook manner performed his assessment of my son's injury. The visit revealed a hairline fracture to his finger that required a finger splint and another long visit to the doctor. After leaving his office, we stopped at radiology to get an appointment for the next day, because Dr. Mack wanted another X-ray of Jarrod's finger the following day. Then we returned home.

When we returned home, Andrew was waiting for us. He was in a lot of pain and his arm had swollen beyond recognition. I took Jarrod to his room and took Andrew back to the same after-hours physician. During this subsequent visit, his short arm cast was bivalved, and he immediately felt relief.

By the time we returned from the cast room to the doctor's office, I noticed that the doctor was quite rude. After making several comments about my sons and their proneness to accidents, he made it very clear that I was interrupting his rest. As he continued with other rude remarks, I felt that his attempt to care for my sons was lacking an element of compassion. It was at that point that I heard Dr. Mack utter his last crude remark. He said, "Would you care for a prescription for your other son? That way, I will not be awakened again."

Sensing what I felt was insensitivity to my children and my life in general, I responded in a similarly rude manner. Staring deeply into his eyeballs, and with tearful eyes, I replied, "Dr. Mack, if my other son is to complain of pain, I am going to bring him back to the Naval Hospital and ask for you by name."

In the same rude manner, I also told him, "You are being paid to be on call. In addition, I feel that if you are able to sleep while you are on call, your salary needs to be adjusted." I heard no rebuttal from the doctor.

In my rude manner, I continued to look at the face of the doctor. Then I remembered a story my grandmother, Simona, told me concerning rudeness and rude people. She said that rudeness was a road that leads us to disharmony. It is a long, addictive road with many inclines along the way. Although we travel this road by choice, our anger, hatred, and revenge are always motivators for selecting it. She ended by saying, "Alexandra, don't let anyone take you along that road." With that recollection, I began to see the compassion that was missing from the doctor's original comments. When his facial appearance began to soften, I thanked him for the care he had given my children and left. We left the doctor's office, stopped for a few minutes to fill Andrew's prescription for pain and then returned home.

When we arrived home, everyone was in bed and our dinner was warming in the oven. We ate, I helped Andrew prepare for the following day and after he went to bed, I took a warm bath. Then I dressed for bed and prepared my clothing for the next day. Taking advantage of the fact that the house was quiet, I went downstairs to my living room. When I looked at the clock in the living room, the time was midnight. I sat down on the living room couch to unwind and meditate, and began by invoking a prayer. I was feeling very tired, but also felt much gratitude because my children were resting and apparently without any discomfort.

Within seconds, after I finished the prayer, my conscious mind was traveling through space, as it often did in my conscious dreamlike visions. The traveling sensation was in a conscious and tremendously fast manner. It felt as if I were hurling my whole body through a vast space.

At the speed I was traveling, I could hear the rush of air hitting loudly against my ears during the moments I spent in flight. In this dreamlike vision, I found myself traveling to a distant place of a familiar scent. By a sudden drop of consciousness in a place I had never seen, I knew I had arrived. There was a sudden stop in the sensation of traveling, and my entire body felt the serene and tranquil surrounding space it now occupied. When I became acclimated to the surrounding space, it felt like one of those summer days that follow the first frosts of late autumn. The air was mild, warm, and hazy, which reminded me of what we in the North American continent call an Indian summer. In my immediate vicinity, I could see that it was early in the evening and the sun had relinquished its space to a beautiful early Indian summer moon. I felt as if all I had to do was breathe in order to be alive.

I turned to see the immediate vicinity and saw that there was a group of people apparently preparing for a meditation. Each person was sitting on a heavy mat on top of a larger fabric that covered the entire floor. The fabric was soft, light, and shone like silk, yet it had a metallic roughness to it. This fabric first called my attention to their legs. Along with the fabric covering the floor, I was mostly intrigued by the odd sitting position of their legs. Their legs appeared to be bending upward and into the heavy mat. Oblivious of my presence, the group of people appeared to be engrossed in preparation for an activity. From my peripheral vision, I saw that a figure immediately stood and walked toward where I was standing. In my excitement, I turned my head in that direction and saw a woman coming toward me. She had a face I had seen before, but I felt it was all in my mind. The woman appeared to recognize me, and my heart began to anticipate our reunion the closer she got. As she got closer, I noticed that she had the most beautiful bluish-gray eyes I had ever seen. When she was finally directly in front of me, I saw her as someone I knew, but I could not recall from where. Then she greeted me and identified herself as one of my family members.

The woman wore an orange dress with a darker orange cord around the waist—similar to the knotted cord girdling the order's habit of the Franciscan friar—and dark-brown sandals. Small white flowers resembling baby's breath adorned her hair. On the crown of her head, she wore a yellow scarf that extended beyond her shoulders and above her waist. In the reflection of the moon, her face had a bluish cast and her light-brown hair had a golden glow. Her entire body vibrated with a sound I had heard before, and I felt that I had known her forever. When she spoke to me, I was surprised to hear the soft melodic voice say, "Welcome! I was expecting you." For the sake of clarity I will refer to this woman by the name "Victoria."

The physical features of Victoria and her soft melodic voice were very familiar to me. I knew she was someone I had met before. In my surprise, I glanced quickly at the group of people to see if there were any other familiar faces among them. The people were sitting on the floor across a wall a short distance from me. Their attention was on the activity and something I could not see from where I was standing. From my vantage point, it appeared to me that in front of them was a person guiding them. My inner intuitive self told me that they had something momentous to show me. In my bewilderment, I was eager to see what they were doing. In the interim, out of nowhere, two other women appeared and joined us. When Victoria asked me to follow her, I did, and as we walked, the other two women followed along.

While walking along a pathway, I noticed that close to Victoria was a formless energy that appeared to be surrounding her entire body.

Victoria walked with a straight spine, as if to show that the extra weight upon her back was heavy. She gave me the impression that to exist and live as a formless, invisible energy was her mission. I strongly sensed that she had a mind mostly designed for thinking heartily of people in times of physical stress, mental confusion and states of psychological and/or physical disease. In the formless energy surrounding her was a vibratory form of clear yellow light inside a white electric matter whose periphery was sealed with a radiating streak of deep orange light. Because of its sound when Victoria spoke, I sensed that she seemed to be aware that the formless energy was there.

Along the pathway, Victoria in her soft, melodic voice told me a story of her family. During the time she spoke, I found myself gazing at her peaceful eyes; in the vision, my sense of time came to a halt. In her story was an amazing, invisible, formless vibration that she called "The Tingling."

The story had a certain appeal to me and I asked her, "What part of our existence is real?"
"That remembered," she replied, "was an illuminating source in the life I led."

In a prying and inquisitive manner, my next question to her was, "Have I lived that part of the vision in this existence, and moreover, if so, how?" The explanation she gave me made no sense to me, and as if realizing this, Victoria continued to talk while walking along the pathway.
Then she said, "This vision lets (it) be the person that enhances as its self listens."
I understood that to mean that as we spoke, I was living that part of the vision. The explanation felt as if the center of my being had given me a convincing analysis for the presence of The Tingling.

The formless energy around Victoria's body was visible to me as a human. In retrospect, this part of the vision was conveying a heartfelt feeling of my conscious awareness to find out what was surrounding my own body at times.

"What is The Tingling energy?" I ardently asked her.
"The Tingling," she replied, "makes the voice come alive."
Close to her was another woman with long skinny arms who said, "The Tingling energy has a human personification."
"I am a human," the other woman said. "My voice is within The Tingling. It is The Tingling, that gives life to the voice," she added This explanation satisfied me. In my mind, I was becoming comfortable with their pattern of speech as well as their source of sound. When they spoke, their arms were using words that I understood.

We continued to walk along the pathway until we came to where Victoria wanted to go, and then she closed the pathway with a hand gesture and—what appeared to be—a three-syllable sound that said "MORRAR". Walking in another direction along another well-paved road, I spotted a handful of coins. I stopped walking and asked how I could carry them, because I wanted to pick them up, and Victoria told me to put them in a cup. When I bent down to take a closer look I noticed that the coins were covered with a lot of dirt. Upon scratching the surface of the dirt-covered coins, I discovered that they had faces imprinted upon them, such as the ones found on religious medallions.

When the three women saw the dirt-covered medals, although they said nothing, their reaction was one of comfort and relief. Then Victoria continued to walk along the paved road and motioned for me to follow. Along the pathway, she continued the story of her family with an explanation of why they were looking at the medals.

While I carried the cup with the medals, she said that by wearing the medals the individual is in touch with himself. From the discussion about the medals, Victoria gave me a lesson on a specific law, and I became fascinated by it. The law showed me that the being with personal growth and learned imagination, whose mind was forming The Tingling, is the human whose face appeared on the medals. I was amazed to hear that I was a member of The Tingling family that had lived as Victoria. What I perceived to be The Tingling family had lived around me forever, now that family had been identified. Perhaps Victoria felt familiar to me because she was I. The walk, in what she said was heaven, felt like I was a tourist who had entered into a deep meditation within herself.

On the surface, their human forms and physical features were similar to mine; however, their physical bodies responded differently from my own. The most striking difference was in the hands and head, which appeared to have other functions. For example, as I was walking along the pathway with Victoria, I spotted a cup. When I went to get the dirt-covered medals to soak them, she said, "Take your gaze and move it to the human form." I picked up the medals with my cupped hands, turned my gaze toward the voice of Victoria, and subsequently when we went to get the cup, my hands were empty and the medals were already in it. In addition, the dirt-covered medals were moist with fluid, as if someone else had scrubbed them ahead of time. Her explanation was: "You have created a pathway that has penetrated into your being."

During the rest of the journey, Victoria remained silent as we followed her through what appeared to be an unending dirt road. After a long walk, we came to a fork in the road, and she led us to the left side of the road toward a group of people. When she veered left, the next thing that happened was very strange; although we had physically walked the long paved road, within an instant, we were sitting with the group.

While sitting with the group, I glanced at myself and noticed that my clothing had changed. The clothes I was wearing had instantly disappeared, as well as the dirt-covered medals I held within my hands. I also noticed that my appearance had transformed into a being that resembled the ones in the group. A total transformation included all of us. Along with the woman who traveled with me, I was wearing a deep pinkish-red gown, navy-blue shawl and navy-blue sandals, and a deep celestial-blue headband around my forehead. All these changes took place when Victoria veered to the left.

The group of people welcomed us with a hand gesture and verbally saying a word. During their utterance of that word, I saw a six-sided symbol shining from their fingers. I also saw that on the sleeves of their gowns they were wearing the same symbols, similar to the ones found in a family crest. Without counting the women traveling with me, I knew there were twenty-one people in the group. Across from me, in a chair that had three legs, sat Victoria, who appeared to be heading the group in an activity in which everyone's body was creating the same vibrating sound.

Forming a circle, each of us sat on a similar three-legged chair, with our bodies facing Victoria. The figure created from our bodies appeared as one invisible form in a linked chain. Lacking the explanations for being alive and having many questions about it, I felt unsuccessful at understanding their language. The sound of her voice had a most peculiar melodic tone that appeared to be spoken with the mouth yet emitted through her hands. It almost seemed as if she was a human being with the vocal cords in her arms. In my conscious awareness, I was very confused while she spoke. I wanted to look at her face, but the source of her voice was coming from her hands, thus pulling my gaze downward. In my confusion, I was unsure where to place my gaze.

From afar, I saw several children walking toward me and felt their tranquility as they were approaching. They had the same symbols on their sleeves as I did. When the children were close to me, they greeted me in the same manner as the people from the group. Following their example, I tried to mimic the salutation that I had previously witnessed. Before I asked, Victoria said, "This salutation is keeping The Tingling family alive. It is a sign that the individual is a personification of The Tingling energy force." I noticed that when the children arrived, their extended fingers projected the image of the medal's existing form. In the story Victoria told us, "The children clothed with the medals," she said, "were personifying the members of The Tingling family."

To me, the vision had a determined objective as well as an element of mystique. For example, when I decided to walk toward the other children, they continued walking toward Victoria. They walked up to her and said in unison that to see me they were to walk to Victoria. Following her salutation, I felt a tingling energy rapidly moving through my arms and traveling throughout my body. Then we walked together, beside each other along the length of the road.

The children and I continued to walk and play, stopping to speak to various types of people along the way. Holding hands, we went merrily along the pathway, and several feet to my right, I noticed two children walking toward me. Immediately in my conscious awareness, Victoria and I became one. In the vision was a human remembrance that went beyond human comprehension; almost instantaneously, Victoria said that, "Within the vision I was testing my feelings." Although their features were strikingly vivid in my mind, the two children were unknown to me. I then noticed that the children were wearing medals similar to mine on their sleeves. I also noticed that they had approached me instead of Victoria. Feeling recognized, I extended a welcoming gesture, and they responded.

Although the vision felt real, my conscious awareness knew that I was in a place where the formless quintessence was visibly alive. This was a means to communicate with an invisible form of energy. I believe that the current of The Tingling energy I received from Victoria was the means for me to measure how the invisible form directs my human illumination, as well as how The Tingling perceives me. In fact, I strongly felt that her silent, loving touch was the way for her to say that I needed an all-together modality to heal and nourish children as well. From nowhere, a woman, who had a lot of hair, came to meet us. She said, "The two children are beings with The Tingling energy who have responded to you. Their real work in this life is healing other families. Their ultimate objective is that invisible form of work."

"Then The Tingling energy is a family whose members are healers?" I asked her.
Looking into my eyes, she leaned closer to me and said, "I am a healer." The woman swirled from side to side, as if to tell the whole world, and with a strong emphatic pitch and a gentle hand movement, said: "Welcome to your family!"
In a flash, I was standing with the same woman in front of a large tree. The children had disappeared into thin air, and the scenery changed. The journey was almost instantaneous; it felt like the warm fall season's wisp of air, rustling through fresh leaves.
Under the large tree, her hair appeared fuller and undulated with soft light brown curls cut short above the shoulders. She looked very dignified with finely chiseled facial features: a small mouth and nose within a small round face. The most striking facial features were her brown eyes. The iris of the pupils were equally dilated and somewhat uncommon to me; lines of blue and dark green radiated outward from the pupils to the extent of the iris. Under the large tree, the woman appeared to be refined,

simple, well informed and very…very humble. During our long talk, the woman spoke to me about what I thought was her real life. Concisely, she was presenting this work to me. As a healer, she was working with children in a school. Her work as a healer was similar to my own as a spiritual healer. As she spoke, a part of me was alive in the vision. In this woman, I sensed the same love for others, the same learned imagination and the same strong healing powers that I felt I had.

As she continued to talk, I realized that my work as a nurse was important and that I was walking the pathway. Imagine the astounding surprise and serendipitous way to hear that one is following along the pathway of the past. It was, to say the least, a tremendously motivating method to communicate. I silently asked myself if this were possible or at least plausible.

Then in amazement, I asked, "Did you ever tell me this story before?" "Why are you expressing a part of this existence?" she replied, as if to say, "Yes!"

I wondered and asked myself how an invisible form could create a visible story, and surmised that said question could be answered but only by asking another question.
"Is this vision a figment of my imagination? On the other hand, is it real?"

The response to this question came in the form of light. When I attempted to ask her, the woman began to glow rapidly until there was nothing but light and I could not visually see her or feel her presence. After my eyes accommodated to the luminosity of the light, its vastness slowly diminished. When the light slowly dimmed to a size two to three inches larger than the periphery of the woman, I could clearly see that she was inside the light.

When once again I was feeling and looking at the woman's presence, being able to see her inside the light was the way to say that she was made-up of light. Had she been a figment of my imagination, reducing her to light,

I believe, would also have extinguished her image as well as the image of the light. By her reappearance, the woman was saying something to me. I believe her reappearance meant that I was not the creator of the vision. The reason I was standing in front of the woman and within the previous panorama told me that she had wanted it that way. It is this part of the vision, and the solution to the above question, that prompted me to deduce that what I perceived as the woman, I also witnessed as light. The woman inside the light was in the vision. Therefore, the vision was real and not a figment of my imagination.

Under the large tree, the conversation returned to the misuse of a law. In relating to an erroneous truth, the woman attempted to explain the laws of life I was misusing. She said that the misused law might have begun as a necessity in order to live in balance. As she spoke, I related to the part of the law explained in the vision. In her discussion of the law were erroneous truths I was using as my valid arguments. When I understood the vision, the myth of the law, and my erroneous truths, her explanations made more sense to me. She concluded by saying that misuse of the law means living outside of the pathway or outside its field of light. In retrospect, I believe that the understanding of these laws of life is essential for correcting any erroneous truth.

After discussing the law I was misusing, the woman walked to the back of the large tree, and I followed her. Along the way, she continued to speak, but this time the topic of discussion was about the pathway.

The woman began by saying that the applicable laws of life are misused if they are not understood in terms of the pathway of our past. "Our life will be deepened with learned imagination," she said, "as we begin to follow the pathway of our past." "The life we choose to lead began in the past," the woman continued.

"To deepen our existence by the work accomplished every hour or at leisure is in part the way we grow. By walking our pathway, the qualities of our life are found along the way. The way we walk the pathway is also a part of our growth. Walking a pathway means leading the life we have chosen in the past. It means that the field of light we have chosen is illuminating our path."

She concluded by saying that when we walk a pathway in its field of light, the law of life is our guide.

As I listened to her discourse, I instantly wanted to know about my own pathway. Intuitively, somewhere inside of me, something inquisitively asked for more. Within me was a very strong feeling that the learned imagination the woman spoke about, in my beautifully verbalized dreamlike vision, was my ultimate challenge; I also sensed that through The Tingling family, my own pathway would be found. Since the woman had beautifully remembered the pathway of The Tingling family, in my mind I wanted to believe that she had also remembered mine—after all, in the vision, walking along a pathway had been emphasized.

While pondering on the above, I noticed that the woman looked at me as if she had just remembered something. Whatever it was, almost as an afterthought, the woman, said, "Your heavenly pathway is what we are walking on. Through this pathway you have walked before; that is why this pathway has a familiar scent."
Perhaps she sensed that I was looking for the answer to my own pathway. On the other hand, perhaps she felt compelled to tell me about my own pathway. Whatever the reason, I hoped she would reveal more.

"Healing others," she continued, "is the pathway to your personal growth. In fact, nursing others, in a sense, is illuminating and carves a pathway for you as a healer. In reality, the compassionate work of nursing others is what healing represents, and you are the one that extended a salutation and responded to The Tingling family. The healer of your past is on this pathway." She continued to talk about other aspects of nursing and I was mesmerized intensely by her pictorial explanations. When the long talk about the pathway ended, as if to close our existence, the woman and I said goodbye. As in her previous remarkable style, Victoria uttered a three-syllable sound, a pathway closed, the entire scenery changed, and the woman with a lot of hair disappeared. In the surrounding vicinity, I heard the sound of blackbirds approaching. I noticed that it was daylight, and I could see the bright-blue sky above. The weather was clear and brisk. In the cool air was the smell of freshly baked bread and along with the weather, the season had changed from autumn to spring. It felt like an early morning spring day.

Once again, standing in front of me was Victoria, the woman with the soft melodic voice. We were on the same pathway where the children and I walked merrily along. Victoria appeared to be walking away from me, as if she had just greeted me. I noticed she wore the symbol of The Tingling family on her sleeves. She turned around and began to walk, as if we were about to embark on another walking expedition.

Although Victoria said nothing, when she turned around I intuitively knew that I needed to follow her, and I did. As she walked in front of me, a continuous, profound sound of peace appeared to be surrounding her entire body. It had the same qualities of the presence I had observed before. I knew then that the presence was The Tingling, and I continued to follow her in that peaceful sound. While I followed her, my conscious memory shifted and placed upon my practice of spiritual healing. During that shift, it became apparent to me that during each spiritual healing, my clients had made comments about a peaceful sound. In that instant, I realized that The Tingling keeps me attuned with the mission I have chosen, and The Tingling's peaceful sound is what my clients hear during a spiritual healing.

My conscious memory shifted once again when Victoria, in her soft melodic voice, turned to me and said, "We are almost there." The shift in consciousness was rapid, but in my mind, I was aware that in the vision I was with her. It was similar to the sensation one feels after waking up in the middle of the night, drinking water or going to the restroom, and returning to the same dream. The softly audible voice brought me back to the activity of walking alongside Victoria. When I heard the voice, I noticed that it came from another woman who was walking behind us. I turned to see who the woman was, and she welcomed me with a three-syllable word. Imagine my amazement when I saw that the woman with a lot of hair was the woman walking behind us. We continued to walk the pathway after I returned the greeting in a similar manner. While we walked, I wondered if the connection were necessary for me.

The response of the woman with a lot of hair was "Yes! It is necessary for the workings of cause and effect." She spoke to me as if I had asked her a question aloud.

"The arm," she continued, "is the real existing work." With a different outlook for The Tingling family, I walked to her and said, "Where are we going?" Without answering, she replied by pointing both hands to the heavens. Along the way, we came across the personification of one medallion I often wear. At the time, I felt that I was looking into the medallion itself. When I compared the image to the resemblance I had in my mind of the face in the medallion, it felt quite authentic in appearance. She looked at me as we approached her and smiled.

I wanted to stop and touch her, but as we came close to her, my conscious awareness changed, and the woman with a lot of hair closed the pathway.

As the pathway closed, I began to have the sense that the vision was ending. Within seconds, my conscious mind was traveling through space in a tremendously rapid manner. At the speed I was traveling, I felt the rush of air as if I were hurling through a vast space. Without a doubt, it was the most beautiful moment I have ever spent in any flight. I knew I had arrived when I heard the chimes of my living room clock. The time was midnight, and I was sitting alone on my living room couch.

In this dreamlike vision, a story of The Tingling family was given to me; it was the gentle beings of this family who listened. In retrospect, I feel this is the story of my own time-space continuum presented and performed by my many life forms. I believe this dreamlike vision was the memory I held of a healing family, along with and within the design of the life's I had lived. From the point in space where I was, I traveled inward, into a peace where I had begun my real existence and ended up mastering my own point in space.

THE WATER POND

> Should you shield the canyons from the windstorms you would never see the true beauty of their carvings.
>
> —Elizabeth Kubler–Ross

Some people often say, "I know that thing exists because I see it." Other people may be more emphatic in their convictions of the existence of something and say, "If it looks like a duck and quacks like a duck; it is a duck." These statements are so cliché that we seem to accept them at their face value.

- Have you ever wondered what these statements mean?
- Have you ever found yourself in the middle of a critical question and wondered if the duck you saw, and the duck you heard quacking was truly a duck?

If you were to recall your early childhood, many of you would agree with what I am about to say. Some of us have been taught that we should judge the world only from our objective impressions of it. Either by the experiences we have witnessed in our lives, or by word of mouth, we have been trained to think of the reality of something from a material point of view. In some cases, it has been ingrained in our minds that unless we actually see a thing or feel, taste, hear, or smell it; we have no significant evidence to believe that the thing exists. In fact, sometimes, we even base decisions on our ability to mentally weigh what we perceive. To further expand on the usage of words and to make us more consciously aware of what we are implying let me explain it thusly. When we say, "I see it," we tend to mean, "My consciousness sees it." The word "see" means that there is a picture in the consciousness. So when we use the word "see" in this manner, the implication is that our baseline data stems from that picture in our consciousness. Thus, it is not overstating the case to say that we may have become potential slaves to the material of things.

Now, in order to explain to you what I learned about the general nature of this topic, please permit me to relate a personal story, along with the personal interpretation and misconception. Having said that, please, let us begin.
This is the story of the day I saw a water pond in a dreamlike vision. I present it here in order that its content can serve as a testimony for the images we perceive. This story explains how The Tingling communicated with me via direct knowing and how this method works. In the account of this story is a message that was given to me by The Tingling. It appears that The Tingling had been communicating with me for many years. As I recall, besides dreamlike visions, The Tingling also spoke to me in many other forms. However, this was the first time The Tingling spoke to me via direct knowing. This is a very interesting method of communication that slowly became another way for me to receive messages from The Tingling.

This story begins on a Thursday upon my arrival to work that morning. When I arrived at work, I noticed that the day was beginning to feel warm. The sun was beginning to radiate from above and the fresh air felt warm upon my skin. A fresh aroma permeated my surroundings, and a silent trace of spring was among the trees. As I began to walk toward my office, I wondered if people who worked outdoors also noticed these qualities of the day. To begin the day, I looked in my office at the schedule for that day. This was my way of planning and prioritizing all the required or mandated projects I wanted to accomplish. It also allowed me to notice any request or unresolved problem a specific teacher was having. In this manner, the mandated projects for the school would not be overlooked, and I was efficiently managing my time as well. When I looked at the schedule, I noticed that most of my school nursing tasks for that day were indoors. Within the scheduled tasks was an immunization clinic I routinely held once a month. That day, there were several classroom inspections and two committee meetings among the scheduled tasks.

Outside my office, there was a line of students and parents waiting for me. Some of the students were waiting for approval to be readmitted to class due to illness, while others had been sent by their respective teachers for specific problems. Some parents were waiting to give approval for their child to receive a required immunization, while others were waiting to bring their child's immunization records up to date. The parents who needed to update their child's immunization record were given the forms to do so, while the other parents were signing permission slips. Meanwhile, the students who needed to be readmitted to class or were sent by a teacher were being checked so they could return to their respective classrooms. After everyone was served, I prepared my schedule for the day.

It began with several classroom inspections, followed by the immunization clinic, and ended with two committee meetings. In my office, as I prepared myself for the classroom inspections, I continued to visualize that beautiful day. All things considered, the day had been full and eventful. I was able to accomplish all I had scheduled for that day. Although I remained very busy, working throughout the day, the time appeared to pass quickly. Yet, it felt as if the day were longer than eight hours, since I had accomplished more than what was in the schedule. When I left my office that day, I felt I had put in a good and meaningful day's work. On my way home, I began to notice the day once again. The sun had retired into the horizon, and the distance was beginning to interfere with its warmth. During this change, it felt as if the sun were out of sight. The sky was full of thick, electric white clouds that appeared to be prophesizing the early signs of a heavy and fruitful rainy day. This was my clue to drive straight home and leave the grocery shopping for another day. Once I arrived home, the daily activity of cooking made me forget the tremendous amount of work I had completed. After changing my clothes and reading the mail, I helped my son with his math homework, as the other children worked on school projects. Then while everyone was busy completing their school assignments, I started the preparations for dinner.

That night was crisp and cold throughout the house. The warmest room was the kitchen. After dinner while washing the dishes; I had the idea that the kitchen would be a perfect place to read a book. At that time, I remembered that while the children were watching television, the kitchen was quiet and would be the best place to read. I hurried with the dishes and started to read a book while the room was still warm. The book I chose failed to interest me and after three chapters I decided to stop, take a bath, and meditate. That night when I finished my bath, it was seven in the evening. In the place where I normally meditate, it was very cold. The bedroom was the only place where I felt I was less likely to be disturbed by noise. It was the farthest room upstairs away from the flow of traffic and main corridors, so I decided to use the bedroom as my meditation chamber for that night.

Within a few minutes, I fell deep into a meditative state. Although I was conscious of my physical body, I knew that there was a strong vibration within and around me. I also knew that the bedroom was warm, but in my meditative state, it felt as if I were directly under a great big central sun. In the tremendous rise in temperature, my physical body appeared to be perspiring profusely. My clothing was sopping wet, and I felt the material as it stuck to different parts of my body. When I concentrated on the perspiration, I began to feel cool, and my body temperature appeared to stabilize, bringing me to a state of awareness in which my body left my mind.

As my mind began to separate from my body, I felt a tremendous force within them, similar to a magnetic pull. Then my mind force appeared to be pulling my physical body, and I felt a sense of traveling. During this time that I was traveling, with only my physical body parts and my mind, I appeared to be in a deep meditative state. Throughout this time,

I knew that I was sitting in my bedroom but was unable to feel the exact location where my physical body and my sitting space came together or met. I traveled in this manner for what appeared to be a long time. Then everything came to a halt, and I abruptly felt that the physical body and the mind were one. In this state of consciousness, I was taken to the awareness that I had arrived and that the invisible, vibratory, formless energy was still within and around me. In that meditation was the beginning of an interesting relationship between The Tingling and me.

Upon arriving, the first thing I saw was the farthest and narrowest point of a river. The river stream was flowing outward and curbing its water toward me. I could sense that each water drop was peaceful and harmoniously blending within the river stream. The water appeared to be cool, and yet as it touched my body; it felt warm and velvety smooth. Then I noticed that I was sensing the qualities of the water through all my human faculties; yet, I was one with the river stream. During that realization, I became consciously aware that, as I continued to feel with all my human faculties, the experience was becoming more real and more vivid. Amidst that precise moment, a sound was audible in my head. It said, "You are a gifted healer; you are one with the authority within you."

The words were in the form of a thought, which appeared out of nowhere and was heard inside my head. In the early phase of this process, the words were the only source of sound I was able to detect. The words were softly spoken, as if someone were whispering inside my head. I noticed that the words came in a stream as I began to feel one with the water.

When I heard the sound, I thought it was coming from me, and I asked myself, "Did I say that?"
Then, as I became consciously one with the experience, I heard another stream of words. This time, the phrase appeared to be answering the question I had asked myself. The stream of words said, "As the river stream flows, so does my consciousness."
In that meditative state, my mind heard and understood the meaning or the phrase. This time, the words left me speechless, yet something within me understood the phrase, and there was nothing else to say.

For the next few minutes, my recollection was vivid. Nevertheless, for a brief moment, my mind shifted to Macbeth,1 a very famous play I had read many times before. In the Shakespearean tragedy, Macbeth, there is a gripping scene at a dinner party in which a man, who was murdered by Macbeth, appeared to him in ghostly form. The man appeared to be physically alive and quite real. At the dinner party, with the exception of Macbeth, no one was able to see the figure of this man. In the interim Macbeth tries desperately to get others to see the figure; meanwhile, his wife, Lady Macbeth, is slowly becoming more and more irritated with her husband's behavior.

Then, apparently having reached her saturation point in a furious tone of voice, she whispered to her husband, "This is the very painting of your fear…when all's done you look but on a stool." In desperation, Macbeth viciously replies: "If I stand here, I saw him!"

After the realization of those words, I began to notice that the water in the river stream felt as if it were also outside of me. Further research of this topic tells me that there does exist in space certain higher vibratory frequencies that can be easily picked up as sound or as pictures. At this juncture, the philosophical question arises: When we fall asleep and dream, do we not see things in our consciousness? Even when we are wide awake, we are apt to see vivid pictures in the consciousness. In either case, awake or sleeping, it is not the thing itself that our inner consciousness perceives, but a vibrational sound that forms a symbolic image, which in turn is a vivid picture of it.

Then upon closer observation, I realized that I was actually seeing a water pond. Within the water pond, I saw a very well-decorated earthly green center similar to the type one would see in an aviary garden. The water pond was peaceful, and there were different ducks wading in the water. While the ducks appeared to be enjoying each peaceful movement, their movement gave the illusion that they were gliding upon the water. Moving in a circular manner, the water created the illusion of silver rings encircling the earthly green decorative center.

When I realized that the movement of the ducks created a current and that the current in turned moved the ducks, I was able to perceive The Tingling life force working harmoniously among two diverse expressions of life. I also understood how The Tingling was living within and around me as a covert water pond whose stream of consciousness I heard inside my head. A few years ago, scientists would have ridiculed the idea of anyone writing about physical healing via direct knowing. For many years, scientists believed that the energies and powers in the human body were due to chemical reactions with something in the oxygen molecules. The topic of direct knowing was considered to be a "divine" gift and in their opinion there was no scientific basis for its success since the same result cannot be yielded repeatedly.

As a celestial healer, who uses her spiritual faculties in her practice, the topic of direct knowing is one of the scientific tools I use to find where a client is holding disease. The premise for my theory is based on the idea that in nature what is absurd, according to our theories, is not always impossible. "…facts…exists which may mean nothing for others. It even happens that a fact or observation stays a very long time under the eyes of a man of science without in any way inspiring him; then suddenly there comes a ray of light, and the mind interprets the fact quite differently and finds for it wholly new relations. The new idea appears; then, with the rapidity of lightning, as a kind of sudden revelation."

My theory was a sudden revelation based on three major existing scientific facts that until then had meant very little to me. During many years of spiritual healing, I worked silently and asked nothing of what others perceived to be a divine gift. As I began to research the tremendous profundity of an electromagnetic field of energy, my own method of healing was revealed. In this revelation, the personal energetic wave frequency appeared to stand on its own merit, and my spiritual healing theories became valid topics of exploration.

The dreamlike vision of the water pond was, for me, a method to explain the principle of one's life. It led me to my own pathway and gave me a new focus into the life I was leading. The last aspect of my theory on spiritual healing relates to the principle or the pathway one is leading in life. It is important to note that a principle in life can be defined as a thought that propels an individual into an unexplainable course of action. It also guides an individual's belief system and the ideas s/he accepts as truth. This vision furnished a missing link in my theory of spiritual healing. Once I understood the symbolic images of the dreamlike vision, they became an aspect of my theory, and the theory was then complete. The next logical question could be, "Can we summarize our consciousness through our life experiences?" The raising of this question, tells the reader that one is alive. Raising this question implies that one is in this human experience. Therefore, to summarize one's life experience is to describe one's qualities. Furthermore, it is a description that depends on verbal communication; therefore, in the description, the experience is distanced from our conscious awareness and its reality is disclosed. The belief is that in our human biocomputer each thought is created by each individual and as we create, so is our reality. The outcome is always related with our soul evolution. In this belief the most logical questions to ask are:

- What is a thought-form?
- Can our biocomputer respond to our thoughts in kind?
- What is the best method to respond to a thought-form?
- If you were to research these questions a response would be found in this book.

In the concept of the questions above is the answer to a fourth question: "Is the collective consciousness a being, as is the human?" In our human consciousness is a built-in biocomputer that programs every space in time. What the person experiences in his biocomputer is the individual's concept of that program. A human being differs from the collective consciousness in its role. In the human consciousness, the being is a secondary source, while in the collective consciousness, the being is the effect of a secondary source. Therefore, the answer to this question is "yes," the collective consciousness is a being, as the human is.

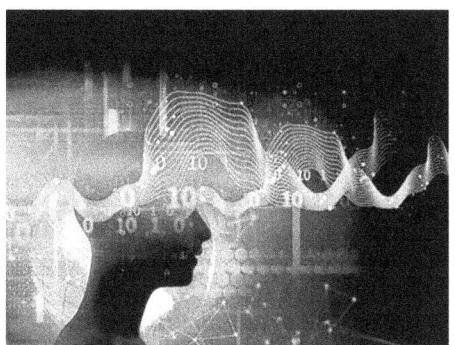

ME AND THE POWER OF TINGLING

The most beautiful and most profound emotion is the sensation of the mystical.

—Albert Einstein

This story has many possible explanations that will be awakened by the reader. I hope it sheds light into your life and upon the other lives you are privileged to touch.
As usual, this journey begins on a Thursday; everyone in my household was commencing their daily routine. On my calendar, I had a seminar scheduled for eleven that morning and had planned to sleep later than usual. When I woke up, it was eight thirty in the morning, my three children and my husband were gone, and I was alone in the house. After having breakfast, I prepared and left the house en route to the seminar.
On the way out the door, I suddenly remembered that the seminar had been canceled. This meant that I was very late for work. In these situations, the school usually calls the field supervisor and they in turn would call the district for a substitute school nurse. I went back into the house to use the telephone and called my work site.

When the office manager answered the telephone, I said, "Valeria, this is Alexandra; I am calling to let you know that I am running very late but I am on my way to the school."
"Yes, Alexandra, thank you for calling," she replied.
Then I said to Valeria, "Tell me, is anyone waiting in my office for urgent care?" "No, Alexandra, there is no one in your office now. We had four accidents on the playground, and Miss Castle (the principal) sent two students home for urgent care. Three other students were cared for by the teachers, in your office, including one that was sent home by the teacher. All the students are in their respective classes now and all the teachers are accounted for," she reported. Hearing about the injuries on the playground, I began to feel the stress that I had caused others and wanted to show Valeria that my tardiness was an honest error on my part and that I cared about the school and its children.

"It sounds like a very active morning. I am grateful that Miss Castle and the teachers were present! I hope those students were not badly injured," I said.
"I don't recall any scheduled gatherings, Valeria. Did I miss any meetings?" I asked.
"You haven't missed any meetings! Miss Castle is making special rounds with Mr. Clark (the vice principal) concerning our fences and the playground incidents," she responded.
"I will follow through with Miss Castle and the respective teachers," I said. "Did you get a call from the district?" I asked
"No, Alexandra, the district has not called," she responded. "And we haven't call for a substitute," she added.

Then when Valeria assured me that a substitute had not been called, I requested, "Please wait until the district makes its routine call. I will call them as soon as possible."
She said, "No problem; I will personally handle it."
After talking with the office manager, I called the school district and spoke with my area coordinator. I told her what had happened and that I intended to go to work. I asked her not to send a substitute nurse, since

I was leaving immediately after our conversation. She agreed, and I left for work.

When I started my car, the clock on the dashboard was showing that it was nine forty-five in the morning. The car engine started right away, and I began my usual one-hour trip to work. I decided to take the freeway, since I was already late. The freeway is always congested early in the morning, and I was accustomed to driving through the side streets; but because the freeway was the fastest route at that time of the day, I thought that the trip would be much easier and faster by the freeway.

I entered the freeway and noticed that the traffic was bumper to bumper. In my mind I wondered what could possibly top that. The way things were going, I was going to be later than I expected. I thought of exiting the freeway, but I knew I would have to drive quite a distance before the next off-ramp. Knowing and believing in Murphy's Law, I decided to relax and enjoy the drive.

I wondered why I had forgotten that the seminar was canceled when I kept a daily planner of all my work and home events. In the interim, the thoughts in my mind were questions of what else I had forgotten. The questions were rapidly moving about in my head, and in the meantime, the traffic came to a stop. As soon as I began to relax, I noticed that the traffic had slowed down, and during that time, I heard a strange sound in my immediate vicinity that I had heard before.

In view of what was happening, I thought the strange sound meant that my car was malfunctioning. I listened closely in case I needed to make an emergency stop on the freeway, but I could not localize the source of the sound. Although the day had started with my forgetting that the seminar had been canceled, I hoped I had not forgotten anything else. Nevertheless, I tried to remember the last time I had serviced my car. Then I remembered that my husband had worked on my car around the beginning of that month. At that time, my car was functioning well, and my husband did the routine maintenance on it. I also recalled that he said everything would be fine until the next routine maintenance. Of course, that remembrance was also subject to Murphy's Law. To be more at ease, I began to sing along with a cassette tape of The Alliance, to the tune of "Did you ever know you were my hero." Meanwhile, in the car, the strange sound was still audible, and I had no idea where it was coming from. I looked out through my car window and in front of me was the strange sound. I saw it as a clear yellow light inside a white electric matter whose periphery was sealed with a radiating streak of deep orange light outside my car, yet I heard it inside the car. The sound had a peaceful undulation that made a cloud of smoke as its color changed from white to shades of an iridescent and luminous orange. The cloud of smoke appeared to be a viscous, translucent, and colloid matter. I tried to focus on the audible sound inside my car and realized that I had heard that sound before. It was the vibratory sound of the formless presence that was frequently around and within me.

Then I began to think about the cloud of smoke I had seen outside the car. During what appeared to be several minutes, the cloud of orange smoke was directly in front of my car; yet the sound was coming from inside my car. Then the traffic began to move, and almost instantly, the cars were exiting at the off-ramp, and I was alone on the freeway. Alone on the freeway, I continued en route to work, and the sound remained audible for the rest of the time I was driving. During what appeared to be a safe trip, I thanked the car for taking me to work and for its perfect performance. Upon arriving, as I entered the school grounds, the sound of peace disappeared. It made the soundless school grounds sound peaceful. It also meant that the classes throughout the entire school were in session. I drove through the school parking lot and parked in my designated spot. When I turned off the engine I noticed that the clock in my car was showing nine forty-five in the morning and the clock timer was still counting the seconds. In my mind, now there were other questions:

- ❖ Where does the sound come from?
- ❖ What is the meaning of the sound?
- ❖ Why do I see a deep orange color?
- ❖ "What happened to the time?
- ❖ Am I a freak of nature? Am I unique? Or are there other people like me?

The answers to these questions will follow.

To answer the first question—Where did the sound come from?—I will go back to the dreamlike vision I described previously in chapter four. In that vision, the woman with a lot of hair appeared when I had questions to be answered. She was The Tingling family member in my pathway who answered my questions. Prior to her appearance, Victoria—the woman with the soft, melodic voice— was with me. During her appearance, I was conscious of a sound that I interpreted as a sound of peace. Throughout the vision, the appearance of the two women was connected by a sound of peace. When I was consciously aware of the sound of peace, the woman with a lot of hair appeared to answer my questions, as if I had asked her the questions personally. In retrospect, I believe that the sound of peace comes from Victoria—the woman with the soft, melodic voice. This answer may seem very evasive to you, but as you continue to read, it may also become your truth.

The answer to the second question—What is the meaning of the sound?—is also related to the vision I described previously in chapter four. In that vision, the woman with the soft, melodic voice was the being asking for my questions to be answered. She appeared to be in tune with my thoughts. Whenever the thoughts in my mind began to ask questions, the sound that was emanating around Victoria caught my eye. Then when I was consciously aware of the sound of peace, the woman with a lot of hair appeared. Her appearance was always related to that sound; therefore, I believe that the woman with a lot of hair was responding to that sound.

In retrospect, now I further believe that the woman with the soft, melodic voice is also in tune with my daily events. The meaning of the sound of peace is related to all my celestial healings; some of my clients hear the sound as well. In their comments, the clients mentioned feeling and listening to a sound of peace. They said that during the healing session, a sound of peace appeared to be coming from me. In some cases, the sound lasted one to three minutes after the sessions. Some of my clients also reported that throughout the silence they had an indescribable inner sensation that their questions were answered. These clients also reported that during the session, the sound was always in the room. The meaning of the sound is a difficult question to answer, and at this time, I will leave it unanswered until further research. The third question—Why do I see a deep orange color?—is still a mystery to me. As I recall, the color orange complements the color blue; the color orange represents the intelligence perfected by man, while the blue represents the perfect man. Orange is the color that radiates throughout the three worlds: the mental, emotional, and physical worlds. The purification of thought is represented by the color orange, and a person with a clean and vibrant mental body exudes an orange auric field. The color orange also represents material fire, and fire transmutes, so this color is a splendid selection for transmuting clarity of thoughts and precision in the presentation of those thoughts. Lastly, the vibrational frequency of the color orange plays a big role in the spiritual healing of several diseases.

The fourth question—What happened to the time?—is not as easily explained. During each actual experience, in all my dreamlike visions, I have noticed that time appears to stop. I deduce from this that while my consciousness is traveling, it has no frame of time in that space continuum; nevertheless, when traveling or actively performing a task in this physical work, our concept of time is still in operation. If that is so, the question—What happened to the time?—still needs to be answered.

That brings me to another question: "Why does The Tingling have a sound of peace?" This question is also related to the visions I described previously in chapter four. In that vision, The Tingling family was an entire mind that perceived each other's thoughts. Their thoughts were heard by all the members of the family. It is similar to the way we perceive other people's thoughts in our minds. The ability to perceive other people's thoughts is the reason I can stop to feel the vision as it fades.

I believe The Tingling is the voice that I hear clairaudiently. In The Tingling is a sound I can interpret. Their symbolic images are the words of the language I clairvoyantly see. Through The Tingling, a feeling of peace is transmitted that my clients experience as a sound of silence. In this silence, the questions are brought to the surface and their answers are disclosed.

Lastly, I will share the following beliefs to answer the questions— Am I a freak of nature? Am I unique? Or Are there other people like me? I will begin this discussion by saying that I am like any other human being. In my earthly life, I have the same stressors that this planet has to offer to all human beings. I have to remember to fill my car with gas, take a bath, take my children to the physician, and prepare my family a balanced meal. Like everyone else, I have to breathe in order to exist. My duties as a citizen are also the same as everyone else. I vote, fulfill my jury duty, and abide by the laws of the federal, state, and local communities. In addition, I must pay my bills, buy groceries, clean my home, and pay taxes. In these respects, there are others like me, and I feel I am neither a freak of nature nor unique.

The stories in this book present thought as a living form that has consciousness. Throughout the stories, the thought-forms are explained as they pertain to my life and in the context of a living thing. In the dreamlike visions, my thoughts became alive and they subsequently lived in my human biocomputer dictating my new behavior. These stories are given in order to explain a specific therapeutic model that anyone can use in healing themselves. As a celestial healer, my work is similar to other healers in the area of alternative healing. The Tingling has been the pathway leading me to my own celestial healing. By choosing to follow this path, the dimensions of my work as a celestial healer have grown, and I am a better registered nurse because of it. Around me is an invisible formless matter that has consciousness. This all powerful being makes me appear as a healer, with the celestial faculty of direct knowing. As a human, I have the same gifts and tool kit that every other human being has. The path that I follow as a celestial healer is also a path that other healers can follow. Therefore, since The Tingling is also within each and every one of us, in that respect, I am like any other healer who chooses to follow this path. Hence, I am neither a freak of nature nor unique.

We are in a world created by our mental images and in a body that responds in kind. Each symbolic image that we perceive emanates from a presence that dwells within us. In our mental images are the living thoughts for behaving in any given situation. These are the beliefs in our biocomputer which drive us and make us behave the way we do. The purpose for these thought-forms at the mental level is simply to carve a road by which we can pattern our lives. In the daily events of our lives, as our behaviors are moving before us, our thoughts can be examined and given strength. They are examined for various reasons, perhaps in some cases without conscious knowledge, but in each case the individual is searching for their validation. The symbolic images are of various levels of consciousness; although their implication may be the same. Since each individual and each human thought-form is sharing the same consciousness, the pattern of behavior can be observed in a visible form. In this conceptual model, our problems are experiences that give us opportunities to evolve. In these problems, we are able to see the psychic myths that we operate under. Consequently, in this manner, our erroneous thought-forms are exposed to the surface and their corresponding truths are found. In this hunting exploration, at the end, the perception we have of any problem will determine the psychic myth we need to heal. In addition, I believe that The Tingling is the pathway I was searching for. The search has been my mission in life as a celestial healer. It is The Tingling I clairsentiently perceive around and within me. By simply being a celestial healer, I carved the road for The Tingling family, and they responded in kind. When I was blessed by their presence, the life I was leading became the breathing in and breathing out in this point in space. I became, at that time in my life, a celestial healer with all the qualities any other healer is privileged to follow. Then in my life, all my questions were answered, and all I had to do was to breathe in and breathe out.

I COULD HAVE SWORN I HEARD THE BIRDS CRY

What though the radiance that was once so bright, be now forever taken from my sight. Though nothing can bring back the hour of splendor in the grass, of glory in the flower; We will grieve not, rather find strength in what remains behind.

—William Wordsworth

This story is a concept of the transmission of pain along with the basic theory for our sensation of hurting. Everyone hurts at one time or another. Some people hurt more frequently and more intensely than others, but pain is universal—one great common bond of this human condition. First, the perception I have of pain is given in portions of a continuous point in space or a "new day." It is an easy argument for believing that another form of life can feel pain. Secondly, the memory we hold of a painful life experience is the basis for my theory. It is an evolutionary theory used as a paradigm for the concept I hold of pain.

Considering how long men have lived with pain, it is remarkable how little firm knowledge they have acquired about its essential nature and effects. The National Institute of General Medical Sciences, a part of the government's famed National Institutes of Health, points out that men

have not even reached consensus on what pain is. Pain is indefinable, except, of course, as each man introspectively defines it for himself.
- Pain to a biologist is a sensory signal that warns a living creature when harmful stimulus threatens to cause him injury.
- On the other hand, a philosopher may view pain as a passion of the soul, an emotional process, and a moralizing influence.
- To a physician, it is always a message to be decoded, interpreted, and acted upon.

Whether pain ennobles the human spirit depends on the subject's response to it. While it may provide heroic examples of fortitude for some people, it may dehumanize others like madness.
A study done by Rene Leriche show that pain is no less painful for being psychosomatic or imaginary in origin. One of his patients was a man who complained of severe pain in a particular location of his jaw. Upon examination of the jaw itself, there seemed to be no identifiable reason for the pain. The attacks not only became more frequent, but instead of being localized, the pain spread over the man's face…utterly debased by pain and fear, he spent his days and nights in despair like an entrapped animal.
Certain parts of the physical body are more sensitive to pain than others:
- The eye, for example, can detect the lowest degree of pain.
- Superficial wounds are often more painful than deep ones.
- One of the most excruciating types of pain comes from the spasms caused by kidney stone colic. Some students of pain believe that a dying man does not feel pain.

Others feel that the sensation is almost wholly. A man during rage feels no pain from injury until after his anger has cooled. The same man waiting in the anteroom of his dentist's office may suffer agony in anticipation. The incidence in intractable pain is increasing and will continue to increase as people are living longer. A price we pay for living longer is chronic degenerative disease. A characteristic of the most prevalent of these diseases—cancer and arthritis—is chronic pain.

Men have made some progress in understanding the cause of pain. In centuries past, he attributed pain to capricious spirits, which entered his body to maliciously torment him. He tried to humor and placated these spirits with elaborate rituals and sacrifices, and he tried to keep them away from him by taboos. By the middle ages, man had come to regard pain as a punishment. It was assumed, then, that whoever felt pain was deserving of it. Modern medicine, of course, looks upon pain as a natural symptom to be diagnosed and alleviated as quickly as possible. For the physician, reading the message properly may be a life-or-death matter. Misinterpretation of a pain message could mean the death of a patient if, for example, a physician was to mistake the pains of a rupturing appendix for an ordinary stomachache and gave the patient a laxative.

The physician's textbook The Management of Pain by Dr. John J. Bonica states that there are two medical concepts of pain: (1) Pain is a necessary warning signal for the body's protection, and (2) pain is a disease in itself. According to this source, pain can be one or the other at different times and in the same person.

In today's society, pain is a leading cause of disability. According to Margo McCaffery (McCaffery, 1980), "Pain is, whatever the client says it is." In her studies of pain are the basic principles I follow. The International Association for the Study of Pain (IASP) defines pain as "an unpleasant subjective sensory and emotional experience associated with actual or potential tissue damage, or described in terms of damage" (IASP, 1979).

In this chapter, we will examine the sensation of hurting we call pain, as I attempt to explain the concept I have of a painful sensation. In an imaginative, creative style, I will present an example of a painful life experience. The purpose of this story is threefold: to present and describe another example of my life experiences; to demonstrate to the reader how The Tingling communicated with me; and to seek an emotional reaction from the reader to the life experience of another living form. In my point of vision, this evolutionary theory is the explanation for feeling another's pain. In this theory, the concept of pain is a sensation of hurting, which can be transmitted through the nervous system from one life form to another. The theory is based on the belief that we are not in this world as the only beings that can communicate. If this theory is correct, every form of life has the capacity to communicate with other forms of life; thus, every form of life has the capability of transmitting, consciously or subconsciously, any one of multiple sensations, such as pain. The story that follows takes place inside my home during the time I sensed two sandalwood trees inside my front yard. Although their lives were lived as sandalwood trees in our physical world, I perceived that for them our world was their spiritual realm. As I recall, I went to open my living room window and saw that it was a beautiful clear day. Looking at my front yard, I saw the two sandalwood trees and felt the cool breeze of spring. We often wonder if other forms of life are like us, and I had the same thoughts then.

- ❖ Have you ever wondered what others feel when they are having a sensation of pain?
- ❖ Can the reader imagine a world in which one can hear birds cry?

I wonder if the reader has ever experienced a visceral understanding of their neighbor's pain. For the reader who has, this story depicts a world that may be similar to their world.

To be moved by this theory, you simply need to recall stories in which animals have given their masters a warning that someone or something was going to cause them harm. In their heroic attempts to save their masters from an invisible harm, they tried to signal their masters with various signs of pain. In some cases, the ultimate fate of these animals was death. Whenever I read these stories, I was often holding my hands together over my face in disbelief.

As my story begins, focus your gaze on a continuous point in space. Now, give yourselves permission to enter a world where different forms of life are having discussions with one another. Further imagine that, in this world, life forms mourn their physical body parts. Hence, when you travel this world, it may be possible for you to sense a part of another living form of life. This imaginative and creative story takes place in my home. It is a true story about my experience with a sandalwood tree.

And so, once upon a day is how the story begins.
This story begins on the day when I received the notice that my daughter-in-law, Rosalyn, was pregnant. I still recall the sparkle in her eyes and the joy in my son's, Jarrod, face when they told me the news. I saw a tremendous joy in both of them, and I in turn was very happy for them; the thought of having a grandchild was, for me, a very beautiful and blessed event. My mind adopted the idea almost instantly, and I began to prepare for my first grandchild. In the early stage of the pregnancy, the planning was giving me many good feelings along with a desire to see the grandchild, and those feelings were giving me an interesting new perspective on life as well.

I began to see my life in the life of my grandchild and the pleasure the child would bring to our lives. Whenever I thought of my future, I was always doing something for my grandchild. Even in my everyday affairs, I included my grandchild. At the store, I looked at children's clothes, furniture, and toys, and wondered if my grandchild would find pleasure in any of the things I thought were cute, useful, or fun.

One morning after completing my routine yoga exercises, I laid on my mat to rest for a while, and almost instantly, I saw lights bouncing like springs. The lights were bright and each had its own distinct quality. They resembled miniature stars twinkling upon a background of darkness. The lights appeared to be flashing on and off in a well-organized rhythmic style. It was almost as if they were each performing for a different play on the same stage. After what appeared to be hours, I heard a voice say, "This is it," and all the lights disappeared. The voice was soft, melodic, low as a whisper, and appeared to be coming from a young female. For the next few moments, I saw nothing but darkness, and in that "nothingness," I felt that my body was beginning to swirl on its axis. It appeared to be rotating to the right and at the same time vibrating in unison, with a strong magnetic pull upwards.

At this time I heard a sound that whispered, "You are there," and I saw myself in a room of familiar scent. Embedded in the walls around the room were several equipments I was familiar with. The room appeared to be a standard intensive care room in a hospital. In what appeared to be a standard hospital bed was the figure of a woman draped with a white sheet from the chest down. The woman appeared to be in distress, pulling on the bed sheets and thrashing about. In order to explore my surroundings, I moved my physical body closer to the woman and noticed that she was alone in the room as if to be waiting to give birth; however, she was not in labor but rather in distress. Upon a closer observation, I was able to see that the woman in the hospital bed was Rosalyn, and then my eyes opened as if I had awakened from a dream.

That afternoon, I called my son and asked him about my daughter-in-law. He was very busy at the time, and our telephone conversation was short but he assured me that they were planning to visit me that day after dinner. When they came, they gave me an update on Rosalyn's pregnancy and on my grandchild's progress— and all was well. I was relieved when I heard that Rosalyn was strong, healthy and had shown no signs of difficulty in delivering and that my grandchild was healthy and growing well.

I asked them if they were prepared with a contact person, in case the baby was born during their working hours. At the time, they were both working days and did not anticipate any problems. Then I gave them a safe, mini version of the vision I had, and Rosalyn suggested adding my name as a contact person in the hospital in case my son was not available at the time of the baby's birth. In my daughter-in-law's suggestion, I saw an element of truth, which I felt was the reason for the vision. I had a very strong feeling that the vision was given to me in order that we could prepare for the coming of my grandchild.

During the time that the pregnancy approached its full term, I continued to prepare for my grandchild's birth. Whenever I spoke with my friends and acquaintances, I never failed to mention that I was expecting a grandchild. In all my conversations with other people, I often asked others about their experiences with their grandchildren and their ideas about being a grandparent. I began to find much pleasure in knowing that I would soon be like all those happy grandparents...and dismissed the vision from my mind.

I distinctly recall that day in the late part of the month of May, as well as how and where that point in space began to turn. Throughout that Thursday I had a sense that someone had entered into my life. In that continuous point in space, I also had a strong premonition that my life would never be the same. As I looked up at the heavens, I saw that a blue color was covering the entire visible space of the sky. I saw how a deep, thick mist of several shades of blue wrapped themselves around each of the white clouds. Throughout the sky, I felt a rhythmic sense of order, and the blue covering gave the heavens a harmonious tone. Each cloud appeared to be dancing in cadence with the same tune. It was a day when I felt the sky and its beauty were part of me, and I felt glad to be alive.

The birds were greeting each other with their sounds of music. Their penetrating chirps still linger in my ears. The birds appeared to know that the day had just begun. Within their continuous melodic tunes, they told each other stories, perhaps of times of yesteryear. I sensed that their memories were filled with many stories of points in space in which their lives had been a part of other human forms. There was a sense of bliss throughout the air, and the latest experience in my life had just begun.

In the air was the pungent scent of a strong, long-lasting fragrance of sandalwood. The crisp, cool air made the odor permeate throughout my surroundings. For me, our sense of smell has a deeper, celestial meaning. Our sense of smell is highly developed and one of our most generous spiritual faculties. With this conscious thought in mind, I recall thinking that sandalwood trees give off their scent even to the ax or blade that cuts off their branches. As I remember, the day had just begun: the beginning of a continuous point in space. In the periphery of my vision were the sounds of photons, which I perceived as light. At a distant point in space was a beautiful planetary body we call a "star." The star was shining and appeared to be accompanied by the moon. Both planetary bodies appeared to be traveling away from me toward another, nonvisible, point in space. I could hear the calm and forceful movement of the wind. As the wind made its audible whirring sounds, its presence filled me with the sound of my own peace profound. When I look back on that day, I recall thinking that the shades of blue of the sky were beginning to respond to our lives with a deeper hue. The deeper color of the sky provided me with a fresh and clear visibility of the atmosphere. The continuous point in space appeared to have ample room, and one could see for miles and miles away. Several species of birds responded to the beautiful atmosphere. They appeared to fly from nowhere. It was almost as if the birds had traveled from afar to take part in a special and mystical event. The birds and their singing reminded me that they had played a big role in my own life. Within their lives I had lived my own, and I began to recall those beautiful times. I remember thinking that the birds were always singing as if they were glad to be alive. The Koran says that as the bird opens its wings in flight, it is praising Allah. And it goes on to say that every motion of the creation is praising the source of creation. It was then that I began to feel a sharp pain throughout my entire forehead. Within seconds, the pain had spread throughout my upper torso and abdomen. With tremendous speed and intensity, the pain began to escalate until it was too excruciating to bear. Within this recollection, I had the strange perception that a part of me was being ripped off. I saw the ripped-off part as having a string of relationships in one mind and in that very strange perception was the sense that I was talking to my closest friend. During this pain, I recall only wanting to help someone. I perceived that someone was a person, and I wanted to be what I felt the person would have wanted me to be.

As the vibratory undulations of electricity became an extension of my arms, from my window I could see the two sandalwood trees and realized that I was sensing the one I will call "Xan." I recall my Herculean attempt to fix my gaze in the direction of the birds as they flew toward Xan. I focused my gaze intensely and tried to see what I thought they were seeing. With all my effort, I began to stare into that open, blank point in space. I tried to imagine a world in which one's physical body could feel pain. But all my attempts were useless…I saw nothing. Yet I could definitely sense an excruciating pain.

In that strange sensation, it was almost as if I were one of the sandalwood trees. I could feel the cool breeze as it moved through the green leafy branches. I could hear the movement of the leaves and I smelled its scent. During the actual spiritual contact, I felt a current of electricity throughout my body. That charge of electricity was visible to me. And then…at that specific point in time, I had a strange perception that Xan was missing a part, and that painful sensation had been transferred to me.

I hope the reader can imagine all the thoughts that came to my mind at that time. The more thoughts that passed through my head, the more questions I had; yet the more questions I asked, the fewer answers I received. In these questions, I felt, were the hidden answers to a part of my whole existence. Deep within me, I felt that if I could answer them, the pain I was feeling for Xan could be localized.

I recall asking out loud, "How can this be so?"
"Is the created image mine?" I mentally asked myself.
The thoughts I was entertaining appeared to be coming from outside of me. They were forming the questions I was asking myself:
"Is the pain really in Xan?" I wondered.
"Is the pain within its mind?" I concluded.
I waited…and waited…and silently waited…but there were no answers; so…I decided to rest.
After what appeared to be a long moment, I asked myself: "Alexandra, where is the pain?"
At that specific moment, I felt my heart beating rapidly, and the chest area surrounding my heart became so constricted that it began to itch. Then, after what appeared to be several minute, almost as a flash of wisdom, I was consciously aware that my gaze had turned once again to the sky. I closed my eyes and made a gesture with my arms—the way one gestures when at last there is no place to hide. I had raised my arms upward, and I turned my head toward the heavens as if asking for and expecting a response. I imagined that I was extending my heart to the heavens and began to say the Lord's Prayer. By the time I had reached the second line: "Who art in heaven," I felt a tear streaming down my face.

Then I noticed that in the deep, thick, mist of several shades of blue, surrounding each white cloud, was an emblem. When I focused my gaze upon it, within an instant, I heard a compassionate melodic voice. The voice whispered, "Xan, you have a missing part. It is not a figment of your own imagination!"

"To sense the visceral pain inside of another is being in touch with your inner self," it continued.

In this experience, I appeared to be speaking and looking at someone. That someone was not of our world. Although I had a sense that my physical body was in this physical world, the experience was not of this world. I also felt that whatever was happening would also yield an explanation for the deep sensation of pain I was experiencing. As if oblivious to this physical world, I traveled to another, while living and occupying my usual physical space. Throughout this experience, I was surrounded by an intense glow, with a bluish- green celestial auric field of compassion.

At that moment, the wind became still and the sky was gray. I realized that the sky had changed in color. I noticed that time had passed and the sky had turned gray. I sensed that the sun had traveled west. I also saw that the continuous point in space had also traveled west. The sky's change in color told me that they were mourning a loss as well.

The thought I had about pain can be described only through the concepts of my own mind. It suddenly dawned on me that while experiencing a sensation of pain, another life form can respond in the same manner. All forms of life experience the same sensation of pain. In this belief, during an experience of pain, another life form may have the same sensation. Pain, in this concept, is used to mean a physical or psychological traumatic sensation. I knew then that I was responding in kind to a sensation of a sandalwood tree that felt like something had been ripped off. My physical body perceived the sandalwood tree, and I could smell its scent—I was in complete alignment with the world of Xan. It was as though my spiritual bodies had come alive.

"Is it possible that in order to experience the pain of another, one must be in complete alignment with the physical and spiritual worlds of the other?" I heard myself murmur.
During my observation of the sandalwood tree, I saw and felt its pain. In the sandalwood tree, I sensed a deep connection with the graying of the sky. I sensed that Xan was telling me that a part of me had been cut off. Then I felt a sharp pain within me. I sensed it was the same pain Xan was feeling. With a strong vibratory frequency, the sharp pain was fiercely rushing throughout my body. At the distal points of my fingertips, I could feel the capillary beds pumping blood through my arms, with a strange, humming, undulating vibration. In addition, it is interesting to note that this sensation was stronger at the tips of the fingers and the area circulating my heart. It was a strange phantom pain that appeared to be emanating from another dimension of life. Yet it was felt deeply and clearly in this physical life.

In this dreamlike vision, one of my most vivid recollections is that while adorning the green leaves of all the branches of the sandalwood trees, the birds, in their pain, were making a humming sound. When I was very young, I recalled when I heard the birds sing for the first time. Although I am unable to replicate their sounds, the birds and their chirping music still fill me with glee. The birds gave me a sense of my inner self, free and with the ability to perceive and capture the given moment. I have not forgotten how peaceful their songs were.

I always felt a deep inner sense of peace profound, when the birds sang… And now…on that glorious Thursday…in my pain, I wanted the birds to sing
Instead…I could have sworn I heard the birds cry.
The following Wednesday evening, a few weeks before the due date of the birth of my grandchild, I had a telephone call. It was approximately nine o'clock at night. When I answered the call I heard a voice say, "Mom?" Over the telephone, the voice sounded full of sadness and very tearful, as if the caller had been crying. In the voice of the caller was a deep pain which I felt strongly within me, and I instinctively knew it was the voice of my son. I said, "Hi, Jarrod, you sound sad. How are you doing?"

His words still linger in my ears. He simply said, "Mom, we need you; we lost the baby."
I responded, "I love you all, Jarrod. I will be at the hospital as soon as possible."

He gave me the pertinent information about the hospital, and our telephone conversation ended. On my way to the hospital, I began to relive the experience I had the previous Thursday with Xan, the sandalwood tree. Now, it was all crystal clear. The pain had been my pain all along. It had originated with me, and now, I was conscious of it within me. In Xan, I had seen the reflection of my pain. It was clear to me, now, that the previous Thursday I had been sensing my own pain.

When I arrived at the hospital, I went to a room of familiar scent. Embedded in the walls around the room were several equipments I was familiar with. It was the hospital's intensive care room I had observed in a previous vision. Lying in the hospital bed was Rosalyn draped in a white sheet from the chest down. She appeared to be in distress, pulling on the bed sheets and thrashing about. As I got closer to her bed, I noticed that she was alone in the room as if to be waiting to give birth; however, she was not in labor but rather in distress. In that previous dreamlike vision I was allowed to see my grandson's fetal demise. In retrospect, I believe that dreamlike vision was a visual dress rehearsal of a very painful experience that was yet to come—Rosalyn's deep distress and my grandchild's fetal demise.

That day, the doctor performed an emergency obstetrical echography on my daughter-in-law to determine the condition of the baby. Utilizing a high resolution Hatachi unit, the gravid uterus was examined with numerous longitudinal and transverse scans. The film demonstrated the following:

- The presence of a single cephalic fetus with the fetal body and spine to the maternal right and the fetal parts to the maternal left
- A fetus that was approximately thirty-three to thirty-four weeks of gestation with no cardiac activity

- No ultrasonically visible lesion related to the spine
- A low normal amount of amniotic fluid
- No observable dilatation of the cerebral ventricles
- An increase echodensity related to the placental region, which was indicative of an abruption, was also noted
- The placenta was anterior in position, extending from the upper uterine body to the lower uterine body
- The placenta showed no signs of placenta praevia, but it was thickened with signs of abruptions

Based on the above signs, the doctor ruled out placenta praevia and presented a final diagnosis of fetal demise due to a probable placenta abruption. The baby—a boy—died in the uterus—and the stillbirth took place forty-eight and a half hours later.

When my grandson was born, I had the fabulous and privileged opportunity to be in his divine presence, and I was fortunate to be able to examine the physical body of the stillbirth. As a nursing instructor, I had a very good understanding of physical death; several weeks prior to my grandchild's death, my students were going through their obstetrical nursing rotation and had completed these lectures. Now the students' questions were more detailed and of a physical nature, and I had trouble answering their specific questions.

I managed to answer all the questions with textbook fluency, yet deep within me, I did not believe my own answers. The reasons given in my textbooks did not satisfy what I was asking myself. I found that the words in my textbooks fell short; they failed to explain the reasons for his death. With my own physical eyes I had confirmed that he was the perfect image of a healthy newborn—I found no physical evidence for this fetal demise. Although I understood the spiritual meaning of my grandchild's death, following this tragedy, I felt as if my whole life had been shattered and I had trouble finding an explanation for the acceptance of his death.

Returning to the dreamlike vision of that glorious Thursday, I recall that the sky, the sun, the sandalwood trees and the birds were all mourning a life form. When I looked around me, time had passed, and I felt their pain. As if in mourning, the sun, in suspended animation, froze its position and maintained a silent, fixed stare.

While weeping, everyone was covered with big, thick drops of moisture, and the whole world was mourning a death. That life had been a part of me. Along with the life forms, I was also mourning my loss. In retrospect, I believe this experience was a preview of a pain within me that was yet to come. The painful life experience I have just described above happened on the Thursday a week before my grandson's fetal demise.

What I learned from these dreamlike visions is that Soul Spirits and their life forms do not revolve around any extended family member. The birth of a Soul Spirit begins with the mission in life that is to be accomplished. It is a delicate commitment between the parties involved. Grace, mercy, and forgiveness are needed in order that, now and then, we can appreciate the miracle of life.

Every life form brings us peace; but, peace is not only found in harmony. It may also be found in conflict, when that conflict is essential for the harmony and welfare of any situation it finds itself, whether alone or in the company of other life forms. It is worth noting that the laws of the universe cannot be changed; whatever is meant to take place on this physical plane will always be accomplished.

The following year, I was given a second opportunity to have a grandchild. This time, the child was born alive, and we were all very happy—our tragedy was over—and I felt that the blessed event was our reward. My grandchild was a boy whom I instantly adored. For some unknown reasons, he reminded me of a District Attorney, and I began to refer to him as "DA."

Sometime later, Rosalyn and Jarrod's marriage ended in a divorce, and I felt once again as if my life had been shattered. Once again, I was asking myself why I had lost my grandchild. This time, the loss was due to the custody agreement between the parents which affected my visits with him. I had a grandchild I was not able to see as often as I cared to. It had been no one's fault; it was simply the result of what, unfortunately, happened in their separation. And now…once again, I wanted the birds to sing. Instead…I could have sworn I heard the birds cry.

"ME" FORGETS WHO "WE" ARE

You are not a drop of water in the ocean, you are the entire ocean in a drop of water.

—Jalal Ad-din Muhammad Rumi (1207–1273)

Several years later, I was teaching a nursing program for the Los Angeles Unified School District (LAUSD) whose entering students were entirely eleventh graders. The program was accredited by the California Board of Nursing, and upon completion, students qualified for the state's nursing license examination.

Although students from any high school were admitted to the program, at the time, only four high schools in this school district participated as campus sites. Since school transportation was not provided, each campus site was strategically located in order to better serve and accommodate every area in that school district. To my knowledge, this program was unique, and the LAUSD was the only school district in California that had attempted such a program. At the time, I was teaching in the South Bay campus site.

The course was given in segments of thirty hours per week, and students met at one high school campus for lecture and at an accredited hospital for their clinical internship. During the entire course, along with teaching them nursing, related mathematics, English, and science, I was their only didactic and clinical instructor. Included in the fundamentals of nursing course I taught was a sixteen-hour block of instruction emphasizing pharmacology and calculation of medication dosages using the metric system, which all nursing students found very difficult to master. As a result, the computation of medication dosages was an area of concern to all the nursing instructors of our school district—so much so that the topic was an ongoing discussion among us.

One Thursday after coming home from work, I was thinking about the difficulty my students were having with learning to use the metric system. Based on personal observation, this group of nursing students was not unusual. Although eventually all my students managed to master this block of instruction, when I arrived home that day I wondered if my students would ever be ready for the State Board of Nursing examination.

That night, I went to bed as usual but was unable to fall asleep. Knowing how important it was for me to be rested the following day, I tried desperately to fall asleep by reading, consuming hot milk with cinnamon, and even counting sheep. To my amazement, that night I tried all the remedies I knew and found them to be keeping me wide awake.

Then at three in the morning, during that sleepless night, a thought came to my mind that perhaps I should get up. The thought came from a voice within me that said "Get up," while from that same inner space, I heard another voice that reminded me how important rest was for me.

Following the voice within me that said "Get up," I got up, and in order to use my time wisely, I decided to work on an old project. If you have ever experienced a sleepless night like this, what follows may be of interest to you. During that sleepless night, I completed a computer-assisted instructional (CAI) program. The CAI program was designed for first-semester nursing students, and it taught them how to express medication dosages as ratios and to calculate medication dosages by using equivalent conversions in the metric system. The CAI program was designed and developed that sleepless night, along with all its mathematical codes, graphic ideas, and computer programming modules. The product was designed to be a supplement for the basic text of this nursing program, and it was specifically written at the level of any high school nursing student. In addition, the comprehension level and the data bank of questions were also going to prepare the high school students for the State Board of Nursing examinations in that area of nursing, because the nine modules of the CAI program addressed the topics of pharmacology and calculation of dosages that related to any inpatient or outpatient client, regardless of their age, disease, or the phase of the client's disease process.

The idea to add music, graphics, and a management file that kept track of a student's trials, errors, and successes was also part of the product developed during that sleepless night. That same night, along with the ideas, the specific piece of music, artwork, and management routines were also very clear to me.

That morning, after the completion of the CAI program, the questions that remained floating in my mind were:
- ❖ Why did it happen on a Thursday?
- ❖ Where did the voices come from?
- ❖ What is the explanation for the sleeplessness?
- ❖ Where did the highest wisdom for that project come from?

To me all of the above questions were very obscure as well as puzzling. They will be explained in this chapter from the level of consciousness that I gained that sleepless night.

The first question—Why did it happen on a Thursday?— I explain as follows. It all started with the Thursday I was born. As I look back on my life, every major event in my life has taken place, has been developed, or has been implemented on a Thursday.
Is this a coincidence? I don't think so! In India Thursday is called "Guruvar," meaning the day of the guru. For me, Thursday has been the

point in space to make contact with The Tingling. The explanation to the second question—Where did the voices come from?—is somewhat similar. Among the voices I heard, I felt that one was that centimeter of chance we sometimes dismiss as crazy. I believe these voices represented an extension of me and they extended my own healing space to let me see that inside the self was a game of chance.

The voice that said "Get up" had more validity and ultimately became that centimeter of chance. In my explanation to this question, I have only to add that the voice that said "get up" was coming from The Tingling. The other voice was coming from my own subconscious belief in eight hours of sleep daily. Both of these explanations cannot be scientifically proven by me. Thus, I will leave it up to the reader to come up with a better explanation. When I asked myself the next question—What is the explanation for the sleeplessness?—at that time, I had no noteworthy or sagacious answer. But today I feel that the sleepless night was a way of working with The Tingling on a project that was to be used with many of my students. The project, I believe, was desperately needed by my students, and the time was ripe for the project.

The last question—Where did the highest wisdom for that project come from?—is also related to The Tingling. This question was unanswered for many years, but today I believe that in the second aspect of my conceptual theory of a cell pattern of disharmony is the answer to this question.

The second aspect is the many bodies of men and women in all dimensions. In Western medicine, healing a person implies that a part of the physical body is in need of cure and/or repair. In our Western belief the many bodies of men and women are not a common practice. This aspect is more acceptable in Eastern medicine. In this theory, there are seven spiritual bodies, one physical body, and one body in a state of finely connected particles of matter. Each body is a replica of the others, having identical anatomy and physiology. The bodies are inside one another. Three of the spiritual bodies are in front of the physical body and four behind it. The remaining body forms an ether in which each body can have existence with its particles of matter.

In this conceptual theory, the bodies are in complete alignment when they are in a state of physical and psychological harmony. The same specific purpose for being is in each body, and each body will respond to disease in the level of understanding that has been accepted as truth. Pain, for example, can be felt in the physical body, although it may be located in one of the other bodies. Because each body resides in a different plane and dimension, the relief of a physical and/or psychological symptom may not necessarily mean a release of disease. Hence, in this theory, a disease will continue to thrive when the disharmony is not visible or physically detectable. In this concept, the reason why all the bodies are not visible to the naked eye can be explained by the sun's white light. My theory posits that everything in the universe is subject to an explanation. In the case of the sun's white light, the laws and theories of the science of physics have scientifically proven its existence and its properties. The sun brings light from east to west, and a beam of it is observed in the physical world with the naked eye. When the beam of light is further examined—as first examined by Sir Isaac Newton in 1666—the findings show that the sun's white light is a mixture of colors. In various studies, this beam of light has been researched by physicists. Their findings have disclosed a moving stream of particles having the properties of color, wave motion, magnetism, electricity, wave length, and frequency within its spectrum.

Furthermore, the physicists found that at the two extremes of the sun's beam of light are ranges of ultraviolet and infrared spectrums not visible by the naked eye. Hence, the beam of light visible to the naked eye is but a small part of a larger spectrum. In the same manner, just as a beam of the sun's white light is visible to the naked eye and a small part of a larger spectrum, so is the visible physical body one of man's multiple bodies. In other words, there are ranges of white light and bodies of man that are not perceived by the human eye. In this theory, the other parts of the spectrum of white light are within the realms of the bodies of man and may be perceived by spiritual faculties.

Since I was five years old, I have been able to use spiritual faculties to see, hear, feel, and smell the multiple bodies of man at "unknown levels." I use the phrase "unknown levels" because at that age, I was not aware of where or how those symbolic images where coming to me. At that age, through the use of these spiritual faculties, I was able to pinpoint where a person's illness was coming from. At that time, I simply knew that the symbols and images I received were very dependable and that they were the reason for my success. It was in this manner that The Tingling communicated with me, but this was the first time that I was privileged to experience the multiple formless bodies within me.

I learned from this experience that in the living pathway of each human, the process of living a peaceful life is found within us. This experience showed me that I am—with the emphasis on the am—I am more than a physical being. It tells me that I also have formless matter and more than one body. The physical body is always evolving because the invisible bodies work together to hold or maintain their highest wisdom. Because these bodies are invisible to the naked eye, they are not given an opportunity to express their expertise. However, during a sleepless night like the one I just described, all the bodies unite and a project of great magnitude is created by all.

The work that is done during a sleepless night is often unique. Such work often has the qualities of expertise in areas such as music, art, education, and science. It also has those carefully thought-out, unique details that make the project stand out. In our life, these bodies are always evolving, because collectively, "me" is the same as "we." In other words, the "me" in us becomes "we," and it seems then that many teachers and masters with different expertise are working together in the work or project.

Since I am a simple, humble, woman of average intelligence I cannot claim credit for the CAI program my physical body designed that sleepless night—nor can I claim to be its highest wisdom; however, I believe there is an unexpressed symbolic image that we cannot see. It is an invisible formless matter that has a specific function to fulfill. Our physical body is within this invisible, formless matter, and our present life is a specific point in the time-space continuum of its existence. The consciousness of that being is the presence that dwells within us. This presence is continuously searching for the spiritual evolution of the invisible formless matter through the veracity of its thought-forms. Then, when this occurs, once we have reached a specific level of spiritual awareness this essence will become our frequency prototype.

Perhaps the words of Jalal Ad-din Muhammad Rumi (1207–1273) can express my sentiments best. The Sufi poet said, "You are the unconditional spirit that is trapped in conditions; like the sun in an eclipse." I interpret the Sufi poet's words as saying that every one of us is more than a physical body. I further believe that the unconditional spirit he spoke about is the invisible formless matter I perceive around and within me. In the words of the Sufi poet, I found the explanation for the presence of The Tingling. His statement was also a motivating factor that mobilized the picturesque ideas responsible for the manifestation of this book.

UNIVERSAL ENERGY

What is soul? It's like electricity—we don't really know what it is but it's a force that can light a room.

—Ray Charles

Throughout my life, I have heard many explanations referring to universal energy. In my meditations I also heard many profound statements. However, I did not possess any facts dictating that there were life forms besides my own outside of this physical world. Hence, I was unable to relate to a formless invisible life that was always within and around me.

My experiences and the questions they generated became an earnest commitment to search for a vibratory energy others could not physically see. To find what appeared to be invisible—that vibration—became the focus of a very insightful and penetrating independent study. It was in this search that relevant and meaningful answers to my most profound questions were found. The desperate and earnest search led to an invisible, formless energy I called The Tingling.

When there is a discussion of the magnitude of The Tingling, it is important to begin with the different related aspects of the subject. Among the topics on this subject was the one on universal substance. The historical literature on this topic begins with a review of what is believed to be the theoretical properties of the universal substance. In a vibratory energy such as The Tingling, the concepts of universal substance are essential; hence, let us explore this concept of universal matter further in order to arrive at that invisible, formless vibration I perceived to be around and within me.

The four major religions: Christianity, Hinduism, Islamism, and Judaism, believe in the significance of the universal substance. In their holy scriptures, the vital universal substance is referred to as a primary source. All of these religions acknowledge the topic of universal substance and its study is well documented in the literature. In their stories, they tell us that the universe has had an electrical frequency from the beginning of time. It will not be my intent to formulate identical theories to these Holy Scriptures. Yet, it is worthy of mentioning that these books are in accord with the existence of a universal substance that has not been explored.

The Christian Bible calls this universal substance "the Holy Ghost" and refers to it as an aspect of the Holy Trinity. The concept of Christianity is said to have emerged in the era beginning with the year formerly thought to be that of the birth of its leader, Master Jesus Christ (c. 4 BC–6 BC). Christians believe that the Holy Ghost is a part of a higher power called God. In fact, all the different faiths based on Christianity believe that the all pervading spirit of the Holy Ghost permeates throughout the universe. The primal energy of the Holy Ghost is said to come from the very fine form of matter in motion, and in primitive times, the Holy Ghost was considered to be an even finer form of matter.

In Hinduism, the universal substance is called "prana." In his book, Vital Energy and Health4 S. Sivananda is quoted by the author as saying that "heat, light, electricity, are all manifestations of prana…Whatever moves, works or has life, is but an expression of prana…Prana is the link between the astral and the physical body." The Vedas are the ancient sacred literature of Hinduism. They were written in Sanskrit circa 1000 BC and consist of four collections of psalms, chants, and sacred formulas.6 The Upanishad is one of the latest Vedic translations dealing with man and his relationship to the universe.7 It emphasizes the pantheism of the ancient Hindu religion. In Hindu theology, Brahma is the eternal essence of the universe and the source of all things. Brahma was unknown to the older Hindu tradition but became the adoration by the Brahmans. Among the Hindus, Brahmans are the ones belonging to the sacerdotal caste. In the beginning, the Brahmans were distinguished for their mental and spiritual superiority. As the time went by, they gradually attracted to themselves power over public worship, ultimately becoming a strictly hereditary class. Today Brahmans are found in many different walks of life, and they still hold in their hands the mysteries of the universal substance.

In the Kabbalah, the universal substance is referred to as "astral light." The Kabbalah is a Jewish mystical theosophy which was written circa 538 BC. It is basically a Jewish mystical interpretation of the Holy Scriptures.

The collection of writings constituting the Jewish civil and religious laws is found in the Talmud. The book consists of two parts. The first part was compiled by the rabbis about AD 200 and contains their oral interpretations. This part is called the Mishnah and is referred to as the text of the Talmud. The second division is called the Gemara and consists of a commentary on the preceding part. The term Talmud is sometimes restricted to the Gemara.

In the Talmud, we are told that "no place is empty of Him," i.e., our world is filled with an energy force which fills every point in this continuum. In this Holy Scripture, "Him" refers to a higher power some people call God. In my point of vision The Tingling is yet to be recognized as a universal healing frequency. The Tingling, which I perceive as vibrating around and within me, is a part of "Him," and as such, I experience it as universal substance.

The Chinese have referred to the existence of a vital energy since the third millennium before Christ. They call this vital energy "chi." In its simplest form "chi" means life force or vital life energy. It is said to be a subtle form of electricity that permeates every living organism and extends throughout the universe. The Chinese concept of universal substance is deeply rooted in Taoist cosmology. The originator, Lao Tzu, is believed to have been born about 604 BC. In his teachings, the Tao is everything. It is all-encompassing, and it is universal. The religion and philosophy of Taoism basically says that "in the beginning was nonbeing, or emptiness. Into that emptiness, came a thought. No one knows where that thought came from, but it set things in motion. In that first moment, chi was formed."

The Taoist, like the Buddhist and the yogis, regard the universe as made up not of matter, but of mind. In their writings, we find evidence of their practice with this vital universal energy. Furthermore, their medical books have diagnoses for diseases in which "chi" is either deficient or unbalanced. The experience of the flow of "chi" in the bodies of the ancient Chinese masters has given rise to our awareness of the vital substance. This awareness is the bridge that connects the beliefs of the ancient Chinese masters with the healing properties of the universal substance. In many of the ancient esoteric and mystical teachings, such a universal vital substance is mentioned. Among the most famous are the Buddhist teachings, such as: Japanese Zen, Tibetan, and Indian forms of Buddhism. The Japanese call this vital substance "ki," while in India, Buddhists call it "prana." Their belief is that a living system is drawing from that universal substance and giving back to it. Their teachings have led many adepts to search for that vital energy.

It is said that Buddhism began as a kind of protest against the religious and social monopoly of the Brahmanic caste of priests in India. The Indian religious teacher, Gautama Buddha (560 BC–480 BC), is said to be the founder of Buddhism, and Indian Buddhic traditions. Buddha is also mentioned in Hindu text as well as in Buddhic philosophy. The substance in nature that allows the "universality" to occur has been called many things. In this area, the literature search indicates that in the universe, there is a substance we need to subsist. Pioneers were astronomers whose search led them to that universal substance. In Europe, the pioneers were astronomers and philosophers, like Aristarchus and Aristotle, whose search led them to that universal substance. As the story unfolds from these inquisitive great minds, their beliefs have made an impact upon our world.

In 260 BC, the Greek astronomer Aristarchus said that the Earth and all other planets moved around the Sun, which was an opposite theory from the common belief. During the time of Aristarchus, the Earth was thought to be the center of everything. The common belief was that the Sun and the planets in the universe moved around the Earth. Aristarchus held the theory that certain movements of the sky could be explained by assuming that the Earth moved around the Sun. Although no one believed him, his theories became a challenge to those whose ideas he had himself criticized. In their concept of the scheme of things, the Greeks believed that the physical space in the universe not occupied by the Earth, planets, Sun, Moon and stars was a "void of darkness." Their focus was on the Earth and the vast "void of darkness" was unexplored.

The next contribution comes from the Greek philosopher Aristotle (384 BC–322 BC). Aristotle's ideas about nature were the first to offer a complete unified picture of the universe. He thought that the planets, stars, and the Earth were transparent because they contained a substance "also found in the eternal body which constitutes the uppermost shell of the physical cosmos."19 His premise was that "a transparent body has potency for transmitting light, but it does not become actually transparent until light is passed through it and thereby brings the transparency into action." Aristotle's theory was most influential because he laid the foundation that gave others a reason to search for the "transparent" substance of the universe.

After several centuries, in the later sixteenth and early seventeenth centuries, the pioneers were astronomers, alchemists, scientists, and philosophers like: Nicholaus Copernicus, Paracelsus, Gilbert William, Galileo Galilei, Johannes Kepler, and Rene Descartes. These men were the first to lay the foundation of modem science. First came, the theories of the Polish astronomer Nicholaus Copernicus (1473–1543). He was the first to show that the planets moved in the heavens. Reviving the idea of Aristarchus that the Earth moved around the Sun, Copernicus published a book containing his theories. In his book, he deduced that as the Earth moved around the Sun, the position of the stars had to change. Copernicus believed that the turning of the Earth on its axis accounted for the apparent rising and setting of the stars and that in order to see the apparent movement of the planets in the heavens, one had to conceive that the Sun was stationary and the planets revolved around it. His contribution was influential because it was a means to study the parts and the substance of the universe by others.

Around the same time, Phillipus Aureolus Paracelsus (1493–1541) was making a revolutionary change in the minds of the sixteenth- century physicians. The famous Swiss alchemist and physician propounded that minerals such as sulphur, mercury, and iron offered better cures for the sick than the plants, herbs, and roots used at the time. His belief was based on "the theory that the curative powers of the minerals was due to the electromagnetic properties they inherited from the heavenly bodies." The theory of using minerals to heal the physical body is still practiced today for the same reason.

Around the same time, William Gilbert (1544–1603) has given us the next significant records. The British scientist concludes that the entire planet is a huge magnet with a vast electromagnetic field stretching between the two poles. Gilbert was the first to introduce the concept of the magnetic field. Along with this discovery he also invented the electroscope, which was the first instrument to measure electric fields. His work was published in his book, De Magnete.

Next came, the Italian astronomer and physicist, Galileo Galilei (1564–1642), whose concepts of inertia earned him the title of the father of modem physics. Galilei was the "first to quantify the physical world. He measured the motion, frequency, velocity, and duration of everything from falling stones to swinging pendulums (like the chandelier in his cathedral)." His discovery of gravitational fields has been the first key to the magnetic pull of the universal substance.

In the late sixteenth century, the German astronomer, Johannes Kepler (1571–1630) started to lay the foundations of modem science. In his ten years of research, Kepler discovered empirical laws of planetary movement and proved that Copernicus was correct in his theories. He advanced Copernicus's theory by explaining the observed motions of the planets. He found that each planet traveled around the Sun in a path called an ellipse. His discovery of the law governing the variation in speed during rotation showed that the sun-planet sweeps out equal areas in equal periods of time. That discovery became the first step toward a search for the cause of the planetary movement.

At about the same time, the French philosopher and mathematician Rene Descartes (1596–1650) presented his theories of the universal substance to the world. Descartes believed that "all of space was filled with globules of a material called ether that could transmit forces." He described the ether as a space continuum in which a specific point could be identified by its coordinates. "It was Rene Descartes who developed many of the fundamental techniques of modem mathematics and gave us the picture of the universe as a 'great machine.'"

The next contributions are from the English philosopher and mathematician Sir Isaac Newton (1642–1727) whose concepts of mass, inertia, and force, and the laws connecting them, were drawn directly from experience. Newton presented a system that explained the planets' movement in their orbits by the law of gravitation, which regarded space as objective and absolute, and a real thing. The law of gravitation states that every body continues in its state of rest, or of uniform motion in a straight line, except as it is compelled by forces to change that state. By proving that gravitation keeps the Moon in its orbit around the Sun, Newton showed that every body in the universe attracts every other body. Newton's theory of gravitation also implies that a body in motion can be stopped if there are forces acting upon it at a distance.
In respect to the universal substance, Newton said, "All space is permeated by an elastic medium or aether, which is capable of propagating vibrations in the same way as the air propagates the vibrations of sound, but with far greater velocity. Its density varies from one body to another,

being greater in the free interplanetary space. It is not a single uniform substance, but just as air contains aqueous vapours, so the aether may contain various aetherial spirits adapted to produce the phenomena of electricity, magnetism, and gravitation."
The findings of the science of motion by Galilei was completed by Sir Isaac Newton. With Newton's theory of gravitation, the ether hypothesis gained much force. "In the days of Newton...physicists had largely been concerned with the universe as they could observe and study it directly... and nothing in that world had yet appeared to suggest that any such relationship between matter and energy existed."
Additionally, in 1666 Newton discovered that the light of the Sun could be split up into component colors by means of a prism. The light of the Sun is white, and after passing through a prism, it showed all the colors which exist in the visible world. Newton called the spectrum of the Sun its visible spectrum and concluded that white light was composed of a mixture of all colors of the spectrum.

In 1675, Olaus Roemer had used astronomical methods to obtain approximately 2.6×10^8 miles per second as a value for the speed of light; in astronomical work, this unit is called a light year. The result of his experiment can be expressed as: the velocity of light in vacua is approximately 186,000 miles per second or 300,000 kilometers per second (almost 670 million miles per hour). During the 1800s, scientists learned the meaning of the rainbow of colors that Newton had produced with his prism. First came the discovery of dark lines in the spectrum of the Sun by W. H. Wollaston (1766–1828), followed by the theory that color and dark lines were produced by atoms of chemical elements, and ending with the theory that the atoms either give off light producing color lines or they hold back certain colors, producing dark lines. From the above theories came the identifying characteristic lines of each element in the spectrum of the Sun. Hans Christian Oersted (1777–1851) followed next by demonstrating that electromagnetism existed. The Danish physicist, a professor of natural science at Copenhagen, proved that an electric current flowing in a conductor generated a circular magnetic field around the conductor. His discovery provided the knowledge of the relationship between the physics of electricity and magnetism, and the basis for much of our present day technology. About the same time, Andre-Marie Ampere (1775–1836) argued that "a current, being competent to originate a magnetic field, must be equivalent to a magnet in other respects; and therefore, that current, like magnets, should exhibit forces of mutual attraction and repulsion. Ampere's reasoning rests on the assumption that the magnetic field produced by a current is, in all respects, of the same nature as that produced by a magnet; in other words, that only one kind of magnetic force exists."

In reference to the ether, "Andre-Marie Ampere found that two wires exert forces on each other when they each carry electric current. No magnet or magnetic material of any kind is necessary, yet this force is a magnetic force. Thus the really fundamental 'magnetic material' turns out to be the motion of charges and not a substance at all."

In 1833, the English physicist, Michael Faraday (1791–1867) succeeded in showing that every known effect of electricity, such as magnetic, chemical, mechanical, physiological, luminosity, and calorific, was found in the ether. Electrical seems to be the best word to describe the energy in the universal substance, since it has a property having characteristics similar to electrical energy. This is a major breakthrough. For the first time in the history of the literature, the universal substance is officially given the properties of electricity. Later in the 1860s, Michael Faraday presented his field theory to the world. Faraday theorized that "electrical or magnetic fields could act upon objects at a distance because the 'empty space' between interacting charged objects or interacting magnetic poles was not really empty at all. He proposed that this space must be filled with a peculiar substance which he referred to as 'world ether' and which he believed was responsible for all electrical and magnetic interactions." His contribution gives birth to the concept of a universe that creates a force by its magnetic fields of electricity. With Faraday's contribution, our magnetic fields of electricity are now being recognized.

The next greatest advancement was in 1964 from the English physicist James Clerk Maxwell (1831–1879). In Maxwell's, work he explained the electric and magnetic effects of the ether in terms of mechanical substance. Maxwell conceived the physical reality as a continuous field and proved that upon acceleration, an electric charge should produce a disturbance in the ether that travels outwards from the source with a speed of 3×108 miles per second.

In Maxwell's electromagnetic field theory, he showed that the electromagnetic fields of the ether were independent realities, since it appeared not to be bound down to any bearer, while light and electromagnetic phenomena were dependent variables. Maxwell's theory on the nature of electromagnetic radiation ruled out the existence of forces acting at a distance.

In the middle of the 1800s, the thirty years of experiments done by Count Wilhelm Von Reichenbach led him to believe that electromagnetic fields exhibited magnetic polarity. In the experiments Von Reichenbach conducted, he referred to the universal substance as "odic force." With his experiments he proved that conduction of electromagnetic fields is possible through a wire. His findings are that the velocity of conduction is four meters per second depending on the mass density of the wire. In the nineteenth century, the wave theory of light established itself. Light was explained as the vibration of an elastic, inert medium filling the whole space of the universe. Light in the empty space of the universal substance was explained as matter of vibrations of the ether. Matter appeared as the substratum of velocity, kinetic energy, mechanical forces of gravity, as well as electromagnetic fields found in a vacuum, such as the unoccupied ether earlier astronomers called a "void of darkness."

During this era, in 1888, the German physicist Heinrich Hertz (1857–1894) discovered the Hertzian waves. According to Hertz, the resulting oscillations of electricity in a conductor verified that light waves are electromagnetic waves. The work that Hertz did showed that the velocity of propagation is finite. Hertz experiments detected the circuits in which alternating electric currents are rapidly pulsating. He proved Maxwell's prediction that those currents emitted waves of electric and magnetic force.

From 1880 to 1882, Albert Abraham Michelson (1852–1931) designed an interferential refractometer that was sensitive to one part in 4 ×l09. He used the instrument to test for an ether wind associated with the progress of the Earth in its orbit. Michelson collected the data "to find out to what degree a beam of light would be slowed down as it traveled head-on through a mysterious substance known as the universal ether, a weight-less, invisible substance which virtually all scientists of the day believed permeated all the space surrounding the Earth and all the space between the stars…If all space where filled with ether, then it followed that the surface of the Earth should be subjected to a constant wind of ether passing by as the Earth passed through it. However, no significant fringe shift was found."

One of the last discoveries of the nineteenth century was the electron theory of Hendrik Antoon Lorentz (1853–1928). In his electron theory of matter, the Dutch physicist proved that the mass of an electron increased with its velocity by assuming that the ether was in a state of absolute rest and the carrier of the electromagnetic field. Lorentz theorized that the ether was fixed in space, and that electricity was lodged in the moving elementary particles. According to Lorentz, the elementary particles of matter are capable of exciting movement because they carried electrical charges. In addition, he deduced the properties of material bodies from their interaction with the elementary electric particles he called electrons. His theory implied that the physical space (what earlier astronomers called the "void of darkness") and the ether were the same thing. Hence, the ether became a substratum for the nature of the indivisible electrical fields of the universal substance. In the early 1900s, the history of the universal substances was well represented and progressed along the lines of human energy fields through the contributions and the work of more great minds. An evolution of thought flowed through them. Their work in this area is said to be in a class of its own. Max Planck and Albert Einstein, for example, have described the particles of the universal substance in great detail. They have answered the question, "What is this universal substance?" and laid the question to rest.

In 1900, the theory of the German physicist Max Plank (1858– 1947) became the next discovery. Plank discovered that "the size of the energy pockets (quanta) of each light frequency (color) is the same." He believed that "energy is absorbed and emitted in little chunks and that the size of the chunks of a low frequency light, like red, is smaller than the size of the chunks of a high frequency light like violet." His discovery earned him the Nobel Prize in 1918 and the title of the father of quantum mechanics.

In 1905, the theory of the Swiss physicist Albert Einstein (1879– 1955) was the next major breakthrough. Einstein demonstrated in theory that "light is made of tiny particles, or photons, and that the photons of high frequency light have more energy than the photons of low frequency light." His discovery earned him the Nobel Prize in 1921.

In reference to the universal substance, Einstein said that "ether must be assumed to exist everywhere, if we wish to explain optical phenomena mechanically. There can be no empty space if light travels only in a medium. The planets, for example, travel through the ether jelly without encountering any resistance such as a material medium would offer to their motion. If ether does not disturb matter in its motion, there can be no interaction between particles of ether and particles of matter."

The universal substance's forms of matter and their explanations are also found in the concepts of the Rosicrucian and Theosophist teachings:

- The English philosopher Sir Francis Bacon (1561–1626) was the Imperator of The Rosicrucian order, AMORC, whose history can be traced to the reign of Thutmoses II in Egypt (1494 BC–1436 BC). The Rosicrucian Order calls the universal substance "nous." In referring to the identity of "nous," Rosicrucians believe that nous is the energy, power, and force emanating from the source of all life. In addition, nous is believed to be vibratory and dual in nature, possessing both positive and negative polarities." In the 1900s, the most famous studies have been done by the esoteric Rosicrucian order.

Their members have made many experiments by which they prove that the energy in the human body is a very high rate of electrical energy and cannot be measured.

- In 1875, Helena P. Blavatsky founded a society called Theosophy, which means "divine wisdom." The Theosophist founder called the universal substance "primordial substance." On the subject of "primordial substance," Madame Blavatsky said that "the primordial Electric Entity…electrifies into life and separates primordial stuff or pregenetic matter into atoms, themselves the source of light and consciousness." The intention of the Theosophy Society was "to investigate unexplained laws of nature and the powers latent in man." In her book, The Secret Doctrine, she diffused the collected knowledge of the laws which governed the universe.

In theory, both the Rosicrucians and the Theosophists agree that the evolution of the universe goes on, not just around us, but within us. According to their records, they both believe that there is a substance throughout the universe which is vital to human beings, and that the substance has healing properties.

In conclusion, in the review of the literature, the great minds agreed that there is a vital substance; however, they referred to it by different terms. Hippocrates called it our "nature's" life force," and Anton Mesmer called it "universal fluid," Wilhelm Reich referred to it as "orgone energy," and others, as described earlier, had similar terms; and the most recent is Brunner who named it "biocosmic energy." I call it…The Tingling.

It is believed that the universal substance is electrical in nature. This would explain the vibration I feel, and why I perceive its frequency. As we follow the review of the literature, the basis for this belief is explained. To understand this, other contributions must be acknowledged.

The work of the Roman poet and philosopher Titus Lucretius Carus (96?-55 BC) has given me another perspective on The Tingling. Nature and its universal substance, according to Lucretius, are defined as the order of freedom. In a sense, Lucretius gives nature a space to share with its universal substance. "Inasmuch as all matter, settling down through infinite time past, would lie together in a heap," said Lucretius, "the universe and the heavens are nature's forms of life"

In Lucretius's definition, the world and the heavens are nature's universes. He says in many of his works that the universe and the heaven are forms of matter. To give detail, he says, "but what can be and is done throughout the universe in various worlds formed on various plans." Last, he continues, "but as it is, sure enough no rest is given to the bodies of the first-beginnings, because there is no lowest point at all."

The definition of nature, in Lucretius's concept, is that the heaven and the universe are parts of the same matter. This concept has its basis in the belief that nature has various forms of one substance and all forms are at the same level. Lucretius's definition of nature has my admiration. It gives us the theory of multiple bodies residing in the same point of a time-space continuum. In his concept of the universal substance, the bodies align, for they are the same matter. Perhaps the poet William Blake said it best when he wrote, "To see a whole world in a grain of sand/And a heaven in a wild flower; Hold infinity in the palm of your hand/And eternity in an hour." To grasp this concept is to understand the relationship between a living organism and its environment. What follows are the theories I have developed in my own life, along with ways they have changed the lives of those around me. They can change your life, too.

Within the following five months after this research study, I developed a paradigm theory for a cell pattern of disharmony. Finding an explanation for clients' comments was the beginning that led me to the answer to the question "What is this vibration?" The question consumed my every waking hour and became a challenge to me. I noticed that in every spiritual healing session there appeared to be an unknown element that I felt was healing the clients. It seemed that another presence was doing the healing, and there seemed to be a mission and a specific purpose for the recognition of that presence. During the spiritual healing sessions,

I became aware that something was vibrating within my immediate vicinity. I was consciously aware that during each spiritual healing, a strong presence vibrated around and within me. As I became aware of the electromagnetic frequency and its properties, the study answered the question I asked in silence: "What is this vibration?" Several thousand years before Christ, according to philosophers and their well-known literature, the best method to measure particles of light energy was to ask a psychic. In that era, it was believed that light energy was seen and felt by those with special divine gifts. Since the universe is measured by particles of light energy, today the material to validate this fact is abundant. We now have evidence that everything in the universe is made up of subatomic particles.

Furthermore, today we measure the individual particles of light and call them photons. In the research study I conducted, the science of celestial healing is called physicism. It is the modem alternative method of healing used by practitioners of spiritual healing. Its theory explains how one diagnoses the physical body by spiritual means as well as heals it with The Tingling frequency. The science of physicism is a method whose bases are founded on physics. Hence, the science of celestial healing is also based on physics.

The laws of subatomic physics tell us with what probability photon particles will give rise to a certain sensation if we let them interact with us. Therefore, in any discussion of spiritual healing, these concepts are fundamental because they explain universal theories and fundamental laws pertaining to our universal substance and its properties. Understanding spiritual healing borders on how well we understand physics and its healing potential. The Tingling is defined as a formless matter with a wide spectrum of electromagnetic vibratory ranges. At the quantum level, the higher frequencies of formless matter appear to be the body's healing ranges. In accordance with these laws, I make the supposition that The Tingling and the science of spiritual healing have their roots on the principles of physics.

In the book Peak Learning, Ronald Gross gives the reader learning techniques. His techniques are designed to enhance learning. Ronald Gross states that his techniques are "specific tools…with which you pilot your learning, steering your path just as an expert navigator conns a ship." I believe that his implication is that learning is also a question of designing how we wish to learn. If his theory is correct, the brain is receiving the thought-form from us and responding according to our designs. This means that the brain is stimulated from outside itself. I deduce from this that one is learning from the behavior or the design, and sometimes the design is not in harmony with the rest of the body.

I sense that in the near future, the brain will be studied at a level that we have never achieved before. When this occurs, the concepts that were our past truths will be replaced by levels of higher dimensions of education.

DIVINE ESSENCE ALWAYS LIGHTS THE DARKNESS

Light thinks it travels faster than anything but it is wrong. No matter how fast light travels, it finds the darkness has always got there first, and is waiting for it.

—Terry Pratchett

Introduction

The reason I have chosen this topic is because I have been given a wealth of information and wish to share it with all of you. There are times in our lives when our Highest Power realizes that what we are about to experience is more than we can carry and he gives us a hand. During these moments of profound sorrow, His Divine Essence Always Lights the Darkness because he sheds light into our lives giving us clarity and understanding. For many of us, the death and dying of a loved one can result in one of those moments. One of the most obvious reasons is that throughout our lives, we are affected greatly by the "unknown." With persons that have not studied any philosophy related to physical death, and who are often very religious, there is always a fear regarding death and the actual dying. For most of us, the unknown always causes fear,

and so it is understandable that, for most of us, those unknown questions related to physical death and dying would make us fearful.
- How many of you have ever experienced the death of someone?
- And what question, or questions, did you create in your mind related to that death?

In my physical line of work, as a health care professional, I have discovered that people tend to ask me the same questions related to death. The six most common questions that cluster around the fact of physical death and invest it with uncertainty and fear are the following:

❖ Will the individual suffer?
❖ Where will the person go when he dies?
❖ Will the individual receive the rewards promised?
❖ Will the individual still be able to guide young children in the right way?
❖ Will all contacts with loved ones be broken?
❖ What is death like anyway?

For those readers who are of like-mind, I hope that by the end of this chapter we can cover some of these questions...So let us begin!
Every man provided he fits within the normal, mental framework of our society has his or her concept of what is death and dying. Perhaps no subject is more surrounded by superstition and misconception than that of death in general. If there is one thing this world ought to know, does not know, and wants to know, it is the process in which, and by which, an inhabitant of this plane of consciousness leaves the physical body to become an inhabitant of the next plane or of an etheric plane. I make this statement because for the most part, our human race has not developed sufficiently to understand what life is or the source from whence this atom that develops self has come. How many of you have read a book or seen a movie related to death and dying? I hope you have, so that you will be able to follow me nicely! According to many people who have studied this subject, death is but a passing of the Soul Spirit into a larger sphere, or a birth—if you will. At the end of this life,

the ego must assimilate what it has experienced, and in order to extract the best from its experiences, it begins the process of physical dying. So death, in these terms, is the passing out of the individual's Soul Spirit or etheric body from the flesh covering. The Soul Spirit does this transfer during the first three and one half days after physical and clinical death. And death is not complete until this process is accomplished. I believe this definition of death is simplistic in nature. Yet, I also know that it is utterly impossible for a human being to understand the change in which death occurs unless we realize that every individual possesses a Soul Spirit form composed of etheric atoms that is just as much matter as the flesh garment that is visible and tangible. So let us discuss a few related points here.

I am assured by those versed in physics that all life down to the atom, and beyond, has etheric form. We know, for example, that every atom of every grain of sand that forms the ocean shore; that every seed, and plant, and tree, and every molecule of earth that covers the barren stone that makes up the mass of rock; and that every drop of water that flows in creeks have etheric form. We are further assured that in and through the ether, all life forms carry light and electricity and all forms of radiation.

Scientists also tell us that the etheric requires for growth a covering of matter lower in vibration than itself the same as the seed planted in the earth, and in that outer garment, it increases and reaches a higher development. So based on these scientific findings, we know that no life can exist in the physical world unless it has a garment suitable for that purpose. When by heat we break down the outer garment of a lump of coal, when the physical no longer holds the energy, the life, or the etheric form, the two are dissociated. In other words, the energy or life form escapes to pass unto some other state of being. The outer garment, the cinder or ash, on the other hand, returns from whence it came, ultimately to be taken up by another form of life until in time it has been so refined that it will hold continuity because it has become etheric. And so it is true that when any form of life dissociates its etheric form from its outer garment, that life form can no longer remain an inhabitant of this physical plane, and what we call physical death occurs.

Man in the same manner is a part of one stupendous whole, evolved from the ether life in the mass. It follows that upon physical death our Soul Spirit, released from that outer garment, our dense body, becomes an inhabitant of a plane where all is etheric. In other words, in the change we call death, the individual has been refined to the point where he holds individuality. Let me remind you, at this point, that to etheric sense and touch, all things are tangible, real, and natural as when in earth life…So keeping that in mind, let us move into the progression of our Soul Spirit.

Physical Death

It has been my experience in my personal and professional vocation that people become aware of their own impending death in stages, and this awareness leads us to conscious dying. Conscious dying is an active mental process of awareness and preparation for one's own physical death. The word "dying" is used to imply the dynamic and individualized process of the actual physical transition. In the case of a terminal illness, dying is a process that often occurs over time, and the client, although in the actual process of dying, is still alive. The goals of becoming aware of impending death, or conscious dying, are to live fully until death comes and to direct or participate in the death process until one is comfortable with accepting the ministration of others.

This brings me to one of the six most common questions people ask me related to death, that being—What is death like anyway?

To answer this question, let me begin by giving an introduction to physical death. In the physical realm, the signs and symptoms of approaching physical death are the following:

The arms and legs may become cool to the touch, and the underside of the body may become darker in color. These symptoms are the result of the blood circulation slowing down.

The person will spend more and more time sleeping during the day and, at times, will be difficult to arouse. This results from slowing down of the body's metabolism.

The person may lose bladder and bowel control, resulting in incontinence. This is the involuntary continual dripping of urine and fecal matter.

The person will have a decreased need for food and drink.

Oral secretions may become more profuse and collect in the back of the throat, producing what is commonly referred to in the medical profession as the "death rattles." This is a result of decreased fluid intake and the person's inability to cough up normal saliva.

The person's vision and hearing may decrease slightly with hearing generally being the last sense to be lost.

The person may become restless, pulling at bed linen and having visions of people or things. This is the result of decreased oxygen to the brain, as well as the decreased metabolism.

The person's breathing pattern will change during sleep to an irregular type of arrhythmic breathing. In this type of breathing, at first the breathing is slow and shallow, then it increases in rapidity and depth until it reaches a maximum. Then it decreases gradually until it stops with ten-to thirty-second periods of no breathing (apnea). This type of breathing pattern is called Cheyne Stokes respiration. Although it occurs in certain acute diseases of the central nervous system, heart, lungs, and in intoxications, it frequently occurs before death.

Physical death is described as the cessation of physiologic processes that sustain life; a passing or parting; letting go of this life, or loss of life. It has also been defined as a "moment in time," because it is usually over with the blink of an eye.

The signs of clinical death include:

- No overt or covert signs of breathing,
- No covert heartbeat—In some states two flat electrocardiogram readings within a twenty-four-hour period is considered a definite sign of death.
- No response to shaking or shouting,
- Lose of bladder and bowel control.
- Eyelids slightly open with eyes fixed on one spot.
- Jaws relaxed and mouth slightly open.
- There are several steps physicians follow to determine how long it has been since death occurred:
- The leg is divided from the ankle to the knee into three parts.

- Beginning with the kneepan as a fourth part, the limb to the thigh is further divided into six parts, or ten in all for the entire limb.
- If section one is colder than section two, the body is assumed to have been dead for one hour.
- If section two is colder than section three, the body has been dead for two hours, and so on.
- Experiments conducted in temperatures between 40° and 80°F proved fairly accurate in over 100 examinations.

Stages of Conscious Dying

Thus far, I have spoken of physical death. If you recall I explained that death usually occurs gradually; however, the consciousness is centered in the higher dimensions for a while before actual transition occurs. If the one departing is not placed under sedatives by his doctor, it is very possible that at the time of actual transition the consciousness may return momentarily and the departing Soul Spirit, even though partially detached from the body, will give a description of the scenes and people he is beholding.

It has been noted by persons attending the death of a relative or friend whose siblings had passed that at the time of dying, he would see the siblings around his bed and exclaim: "There is Jonnie! What a beautiful girl she has grown to be." The people present around the bed would probably think that it is a hallucination, but it is not.

Certain phenomenon is always related to those visions—when a person dies, there comes over him a darkness, which he feels descending upon him. With some people, the darkness lifts after a moment, and then, the person is clairvoyant, seeing both the present world and the desire world, and there appear the loved ones who have been attracted by the impending death, which is birth into their world. On the other hand, other persons pass without again seeing the physical world, which is the change from our light vibrations to the vibrations of the desire world and is similar to the darkness that spread over the earth at the time of the crucifixion. Or he may become suddenly conscious of what is transpiring and say a last farewell to those beside him.

When death is imminent, it is very important to bid the dying person farewell. When a guest is departing, we see them to the door and bid them good journey—saying our farewells until we meet again. It is well to learn to do this with those who are departing earth life. During this time or immediately after death, if it is possible, a prayer should be spoken committing the body to the four mighty archangels of the elemental kingdom: Raphael, Michael, Gabriel, and Uriel. The rite, as simple as it sounds, surrounds the dead or dying form with the proper force field of disintegration. When these mighty archangels are invoked, such a ceremony immediately surrounds the form with light. My personal preference is the "Our Father" because it has a tendency to produce a peace profound.

During this process of physical death, the Soul Spirit is also preparing for his spiritual birth by releasing its pull on the physical world. There appears to be a process, already in place, for the actual transition of the Soul Spirit. We have three seed atoms that activate the process of the transition: the astral seed atom, mental seed atom, and physical seed atom. Let us briefly delve into each and see how we might benefit from this knowledge.

1. The astral seed atom is located in the great lobe of the liver we call the solar plexus. It connects to the Soul Spirit by means of the astral-emotional cord. The cord is just what each person has made of it depending on his emotions and desires, and serves as a pathway of expression for all the emotional energies experienced by the individual. It has stamped upon it all the qualities on the emotions ever experienced by the individual. The astral seed atom encapsulates all the inherent weaknesses and strengths of character developed by the individual as far as his desires and emotions are concerned. This allows the person to influence his own future or his own destiny.

2. The mental seed atom is located in the pineal gland within the brain and connects to the super-conscious mind in the over-soul triangle above the individual's head by means of the consciousness cord. As in the case of the first one, this seed atom also contains a record. It is the record of all the inherited and innate qualities of the mind of the individual. Within this seed atom is registered all the mental and mind powers, developed by and through the individual during the ages of his evolutionary progress. So, in essence, the mental seed atom is also an atom of the present and the future. This indicates that we can create changes within the mental seed atom immediately simply by changing our minds, because it enables the person to also influence his own future and his own destiny. It is important to note that when the consciousness cord is fully developed, the individual will have a direct "connection" to his superconscious mind and will become a "master mind." I believe that the saying "Be thee transformed by the renewing of your mind" is basically true. The mental seed atom is today what you have made it in the past incarnations. Yet, it can be endowed with greater powers now to affect both the immediate present and future of the individual.

3. The physical seed atom is located in the right ventricle of the heart. It connects to the divine spirit through the life cord. The life cord is the creation of divinity itself, and the individual has nothing to do with its operation. Life forces pour downward by way of the life cord into the physical form and are distributed through the heart seed atom into the body by the bloodstream. It is here where we find the perpetual record of a person's past that ties the individual to his karmic destiny. The record includes the physical, emotional, and mental aspects. The astral and mental seed atoms record the qualities of the emotions and the mind. The physical seed atom, on the other hand, records a complete electronic picture record of everything that has ever happened to the individual throughout his existence. So in essence, the astral and mental seed atoms release the qualities of the emotions and the mind into the bloodstream, while the

physical seed atom releases actual atomic picture images of the past.

4. What actually occurs at death, in the spiritual realm is that the force of the individual's seed atoms leaves the body. The slow withdrawal of the atoms, which we call the "etching of the seed atoms," is the normal process of death. The human body is a machine with the three seed atoms—a machine for the utilization of the energy and life forces that is employed by the personality in the process of spiritual growth. When those three seed atoms and all its impressions are transferred from the vital body into the desire body, which then forms the basis of the man or woman's life in purgatory and the first heaven, the complete withdrawal brings about the appointed moment of actual transition.

5. In the process of its evolution, the Soul Spirit gathers wisdom through the experiences in the physical form. It is only through death and the dissolution of the atoms of your present form that the soul is provided an opportunity to build a better one. Regardless of how perfect, or how beautiful, your present form is, the purpose of the Soul Spirit is to build ever more perfect forms through which to express. So like a caterpillar, we must die and shed our outer covering in order to emerge as the beautiful butterfly. The time required for this separation depends considerably upon the stored up electromagnetic power in the etheric force field of the individual. When those electromagnetic forces have run their course and the three seed atoms have completely detached, the etheric body releases its hold upon the silver cord. Then when the cord breaks, the Soul Spirit is completely liberated.

6. Therefore, in reference to the six most common questions I am often asked about death, I would like at this time to address the question—Will the individual suffer? I will end this introduction on conscious dying by saying that every change in nature is beautiful, and physical death is no exception to this rule. The death change is simply the liberation of our Soul

Spirit form from the physical body composing the outer flesh garment, and it is perfectly natural and painless. Furthermore, since the consciousness is not in the brain, at this time, there is no suffering.

Spiritual Birth

Just as the process of birth includes more than labor, so the process of death includes more that the mere cessation of the breath and heartbeat. There is an outgoing process in physical death just as there is an incoming process in physical birth. Involved in the process of physical birth is the passage of the baby's physical form downwards into the birth canal. At this time, there is a slow and gradual opening of the birth canal to allow the passage of the new form along with the natural contraction of the physical uterus.

In the process of physical death, the physical form becomes that uterus out of which the Soul Spirit must rise.

At this time, the chemical substance of the endocrine glands centers on the pineal gland. The chemicals strive to free the mental seed atom from the brain. Once free, it passes outwards to the crown of the head by the silver cord. What is very interesting to me is that in every human birth process, the sutures of the parietal and occipital bones are open. This allows for the bones of the skull to overlap, allowing the large bony head of the neonate to pass through the birth canal of the mother. When the baby is born, the sutures unite, creating a gap we call the anterior and posterior fontanels, or the "soft spots," of the neonatal head. During the physical death process, the same thing occurs in reverse. Here the anterior and posterior fontanels open, allowing the sutures of the parietal and occipital bones of the skull to open, and the Soul Spirit passes through this birth canal as well.

The endocrine chemical substance then gathers with a great force and intensity around the heart area. This begins the struggle to free the physical body. The actual break or separation of the silver cord stimulates the consciousness to recall and relive incidents that need to be experienced again, in order to emphasize the lessons they were intended to teach when that person was on the physical plane. After the silver cord breaks, the Soul Spirit enters his astral sheath. For the average person, the process consists of spending the next three and a half days following death in a state of what could be called a deep sleep or a death trance. During these eighty-four hours, the person should be helped by our blessings. It helps when our loving thoughts are directed toward the person's enlightening experiences in his new state of life. This attitude on our part can free the person for his own soul progression during the period immediately following transition.

For the enlightened person, the after-death experience is a journey into ecstasy and initiation or salvation. For the so-called, quote, unquote, sinner, it is an experience called judgment. The journey along the pathway of judgment is not actually in space. It is all performed in the consciousness, and it is the Soul Spirit who relives every incident and episode from the time of his birth. This journey appears to be taken alone, but in actuality, one is always under the ministration of a master. In this journey, one watches his entire life in review, witnessing it as a panorama of passing events. He not only is viewing the scenes, but he is taking part in them. So in reality, we stand aside watching ourselves acting upon the stage of the life that has just passed. During this time, our Soul Spirit is awake on the plane of desire and the passing parade of events exposes his personal, frustrated desires; the scenery surrounding the person in his own panorama will have a definite symbolical relationship to the problems of his individual Soul Spirit, his status in evolution and his cosmic reaction. However, the soul remains in this earth plane while the entire "movie of memories" passes before his consciousness. These symbolic images are derived from the experiences of his own history. In this experience, the Soul Spirit looks upon its own image and undergoes a struggle severe in proportion to its deviation from the spiritual standards.

The Christian measures his Soul Spirit by Christ and his teachings. Therefore, the panorama of the Christian will differ in many ways from that of the Buddhist, the Moslem, the Hindu or the Jew, just to name a few. These experiences will depict what might have come to him had he turned toward the light at any fork along his pathway. Throughout this journey, he is shown where he made his critical decisions and how the choice or choices were always his. So he experiences his own repentance for he sees not only the things he brought upon himself but the glories that he missed. The scenes created become involved in the process of forgiveness. The person either forgives or is forgiven and will be held in this process until he is cleared. As in all things, according to the evolutionary status, each Soul Spirit will face a different personal experience in his departure from the physical form and the earth plane. There are usually three types of reactions to the experiences in the process of death.

1. The first type is the reaction found in the average person. This one is a slow, natural detachment of the soul lasting on the average approximately eighty-four hours after physical and clinical death.
2. The second type is the sudden separation of the Soul Spirit through violence. I must remind you that violent acts differ, and in all violent acts, a sudden withdrawal does not necessarily follow.
3. The third and last type is the immediate withdrawal with no break in consciousness, lasting on the average approximately six minutes. This is the type that is frequently experienced by those who are spiritually enlightened.

I began this chapter by stating that I had been given a wealth of knowledge that I want to share with all of you. I will share some of that information with you, but first let me tell you when and how I received that information, as well as its relationship to the topic of death and dying. I will begin this story with a short and brief definition of what is to be understood by the word "Spirit."

The word spirit possesses many meanings. For example, spirit can be used to mean an individual who has made his transition and passed on to the next dimension of life—a discarnate entity. It can also mean someone now living on earth—an incarnate entity. Or "Spirit" can be defined as a form of "esprit de corps" which radiates from an individual or a group of individuals. It is something very powerful, yet also very subtle, something unseen yet having an effect upon people and even on situations. However, for the purpose of this chapter, let us agree that by the word "Spirit," we mean an animating principle of life. Let us agree that this animating principle of life has the following characteristics:

1. It is present in every form of life.
2. It emanates from whatever we believe to be our highest cosmic power.
3. It pervades everything that exists everywhere in the universe.
4. It permeates tiny insignificant particles of matter.
5. It is divine and etheric in origin.
6. Further, let us agree that, in terms of illumination, the light that comes from spirit flows through every situation in which you are involved, either in the company of others or by yourself.

Now, moving on from this short and brief definition, as to what is to be understood by the word "spirit," I will give you a point of reference. Science tells us that "energy comes from motion, and that motion comes from energy." This can be explained as follows. As many of you already know, there are two types or forms of energy: static and restless energy, or negative and positive energies. When the energies of positive and negative qualities meet, restlessness is created. The end result of restlessness is motion, which produces energy once again. This may seem or appear to have little or nothing to do with the principles of spirit and light at the moment; yet, in certain situations, the vitality we manifest is the result of negative and positive qualities or conditions that take us to a stage in our lives in which we would soon lose all appreciation of Spirit's divine light.

The best instruction in our life and development will come directly from the cosmic spirit revelations. When this happens, a light is turned on, and like magic, a veil is lifted from any given painful or stressful situation. Even when the result is a guilty conscience, when the act never becomes known and we do not have to acknowledge it, we still feel the damage to our personal integrity and struggle growing out of it.

If it were not for light, we would not have any appreciation or comprehension of what constitutes darkness. We would be so accustomed to the absence of light, so accustomed to what we now call darkness, that we could not call it by any name at all that would suggest a contrast in terms of light. We would simply call it the natural condition. This is what happens when we get used to a situation that is malefic in nature, a situation that is dangerous to any form of life, a situation that is hazardous to society, or a condition in our lives that is not conducive to good health; be that moral, legal, spiritual, or physical health. These are the patterns in our lives that create the condition of apathy. In this condition, we lose track of where the light is coming from and hence, are unable to prioritize the significant events of our lives.

In looking back to a time when this light energy of Spirit was put into motion in my own life, I think of my birthday. I think of what took place on that day. Perhaps you already know this, but it is certainly true that the force of Spirit in its totality is incomprehensible to our finite minds. But to help me have at least a wisp of partial knowledge of what had taken place that day, the Spirit force of divine light brought me clarity and understanding.

At the moment I wrote the words of the event that follows, only a few hours had passed since I had become one terrestrial year older. It was my birthday, September 11, 2001, and the coordinates of that point in space we call the United States had been recently struck by indescribable horror.

When I arrived home from work that night, my immediate reaction was to enter into a personal space in my home where I pray and begin to privately pray for six of my family members and friends whom I was sure had been killed and ten others who lived and worked in the immediate vicinity of the tragic and brutal terrorist attack upon the United States. In that personal space of my home and within my private inner chambers, I asked in silence for light to be shed upon our lives. I wanted to know the status of the scheme of things.

Many words were spoken and many things took place that I cannot clearly describe. Perhaps, I deliberately shut off my spiritual vision in order not to see the thousands of dead bodies. Or was it perhaps that I deliberately turned off my spiritual hearing in order not to hear the laments and sorrows of thousands of dead bodies? I recall only the chatter of my own voice. During this time, I saw or heard nothing, but I felt the darkness and what appeared to be an extremely long moment of profound sorrow. Then in my words and in my own voice I heard myself say: "Where is your Divine Essence?"

At this time, a bright light began to shine upon me and I saw the face of whom I call my Highest Cosmic Master. With his image came the response to my question. It clearly and distinctly said: "Lights the darkness." Then within a split second, I saw the body of my Highest Cosmic Master supervising a choir of angels. The angels, as well as the Cosmic Master, were dressed in garments that resembled a polished linen material. It was an electric white dress that was loosely fitted; yet, it seemed to delineate what I am accustomed to calling a humanoid physical form.

Close to, and encircling the Twin Towers in New York City, were thirty-two angels and my Highest Cosmic Master standing at the bottom of the rubble. I noticed at once that a braided strand of golden thread was emanating from the heart of the Cosmic Master. From my vantage point, the braided strand of golden thread appeared to enter into the right ventricle of the heart of each angel—from the front of their hearts—and exit through the back of their hearts. Commencing its extension from the merciful heart of the Cosmic Master, at approximately every six to eight feet, it pierced individually into each angel's heart: thus creating an angelic chain that extended the length of several miles of the braided golden thread. I could not see their hands, but each angel appeared to be holding on to the braided strand of golden thread a few inches from his heart's portal entrance. It was almost as though someone or something was moving the golden thread with invisible hands. I noticed that whenever an angel made a movement with his portion of the golden thread, a number of celestial souls were lifted from the dead bodies that were on top, underneath, within, and among all the debris. I also noticed that each angel greeted each Soul Spirit as if it was a member of his own family. I heard them whisper: "the father of," "the mother of," "the son of," "the daughter of," "the brother of," "the uncle of," and so on and so forth. Then after each was welcomed, the identified Soul Spirit attached itself to the golden thread in front of an angel.

In this dreamlike vision, while I observed the immediate surroundings, I noticed that it was neither day nor night. I could not see a star or a ray of light. But I could sense that there was gloom all around us. I carefully watched, and among the victims was a dark atmosphere with flashes of red that appeared to swallow us with a thick and heavy mist. As all the dead bodies waited in a silent fear, I seemed to be feeling their thoughts; I could hear them think.

Shortly after, several angels with kindly faces approached the victims, and they were told what had occurred and were brought to the realization of their situation. When a new fact was stated, the law and the conditions making such fact possible were also explained. It was only after many explanations that each of the victims came to understand that in the crash of the airplane against the Twin Towers of New York City, their Soul Spirits had been forced out of their physical bodies. I was able to grasp when each victim came to a realizing sense that he had left the physical world of men, because when they realized that in the catastrophe they had gone out of earth-life, their sorrow was beyond words.

At that point in time, I felt the sorrow that came to them with such realization. It was sorrow for the wife, sorrow for the husband, sorrow for their babies and all those they were leaving behind, as well as the questioning whether their trials, sorrows, and suffering incidents in the physical world had been necessary. It was also very clear to me that from the vantage point of some of the victims, the matter of living a few years, more or less, was very important. Their great grief when they learned what had actually happened bound them and held them to that condition and that point in space. I learned then that in a violent death of this type, the death may be accompanied by some measure of momentary shock. I specifically recall seeing a small, heavy-set woman with almond shaped eyes and a well-defined contagious smile. When the other victims were approached, she commented that she was "perfectly fine." At the time she spoke, I still recall thinking how much she reminded me of someone I knew. The woman did not realize that her physical form had been killed and that she was dead to the physical plane. However, the sight of her stricken physical body, surrounded by other dead bodies, was the means of her eventual realization.

What happened in this case was that previous to the airplane striking the Twin Towers, the heart seed atom released the picture images of her approaching death into the bloodstream, and the endocrine glands of this woman suddenly secreted their transitional hormones. At this time, the other two seed atoms in the physical form became prepared to be released from the physical form. As a consequence, our Higher Power's mercy comes into play, and the instantaneous secretion into the bloodstream causes a temporary suspension of consciousness. The deep sleep of death that follows is no more than an anesthetic at work in the body. It blocks the waking consciousness for a given time, closing off the conscious awareness of the Soul Spirit while the higher forms and spiritual forces are separated or withdrawn. As a result, the shock of the sudden projection of the astral-mental body from the physical form is not registered in the mind, so after the impact, the spiritual body was jarred free of the physical, and the woman continued her last conscious thought as if there had been no fatal blow at all.

The victims remained in this state for what appeared to me to be a long while. Then several angels with kindly faces began to speak out loud. This time, their words were not imprinted in a mental picture as before. This time, it was almost as if my ears were recording specific patterns of human speech. They told the victims that their "death had only advanced their sphere of life; and that they were still living beings, inhabitants now of the first plane beyond the earth…" After a few other comments, they ended by saying that "only through physical death could each of them progress." I noticed that throughout the contact, the victims did not move. I sensed that they did not find happiness until the time that the angels had spoken to them. Somehow, the presence of the angels, or perhaps the angels' words themselves, had healed their particular sorrows. Once they came to full consciousness, they were able to move at will. Then the dark condition seemed to change before my eyes, just as mist dissolves before the sun, and a ray of light that grew brighter each moment replaced it.

The terrorists appeared to be together in a heaped pile. When I counted the bodies, there were ten terrorists. Among them were two victims who had been part of the same group of terrorists. The group of bodies I saw was placed in the same actual space of the braided strand of golden thread. Their position or placement between the same two angels seemed to indicate that their final destination was also the same place. Although they appeared to be isolated from the victims in a heaped pile, the angels approached the terrorists in the same manner. I was not able to see, hear, or perceive any differential treatment. The angels welcomed and treated the terrorists in the same loving, humble manner with which they had served the victims.

For the terrorists, it was substantially the same appearance that prevailed with the victims. Yet for the terrorists who perished that day, the same emanations appeared to be producing a different effect. The most intense was their tangibility, which was uttered by the dark and red ether around them itself.... The extent of which you have no idea. This is one experience I want to relate because it has made a profound impression upon me. For a moment, the first apparent difference was that within the terrorists, there was no unconscious state. They were not thinkers; they drifted almost as if they had no mental faculties. Furthermore, even though I could sense that they felt the suffering of humanity—a mother's mourning, a wife's heart breaking, a child sobbing—the thought suggestions I was sensing appeared to help and sustain the terrorists with a virility and vigor. In that force, they seemed to satisfy a greed inhabited by what I understood as raw selfishness. It was presented to me as an ambition giving them the authority to defend a nation or the integrity of a country in a divine order. I had a distinct impression that although they knew their end result was physical death, they had clues as to the understanding of physical death. It was not a simple understanding of what physical death was, but a deeper understanding of what the death of all led to. In the reality about them, there was no fear. For them, living in the present time was not as intense as it was for the victims. In the presence of such an experience, I could see how they had released the pull of the physical realm.

With my Christian background, I was hoping and perhaps expecting a small glimpse of remorse. I wanted to hear the terrorists, the angels, or someone, say they were sorry. I wanted to hear that some good might come out of it—but I heard nothing like this. Soon, above them, arose a golden cloud that formed and moved as if directed. When I asked in my mind, I was told, or had a sense that I was told, that the terrorists were concentrating their thoughts. Yet, what was over them was not emanating from their own thoughts. With a pure, undiluted hungry ambition, they appeared to be communicating with the God force within them.

The angels with kindly faces also came to the terrorists as a ray of light that grew larger by the moment, and I listened to the stream of words of encouragement that flooded into my mind. The words were:

"We are taught about the love of a Higher Power as soon as we are able to accept the new conditions of life after death. He is not the abstract Divine Force that most humans on earth know. We must recognize that this Higher Power is at the heart of everything. He is the one power that flows through all creation. You can only truly know yourself when you understand that this Divine Force is the only well from which you can draw the water of life. There is no other source when we have this mental concept of a Higher Power."

I realized then that we are taught how to draw on his power. However, until then, we are not left on our own in an objective world. It may appear objective to us, but it has been created by the intangible mind of a Higher Power with his will flowing through every image of his creation and giving life to all. At this time, I also realized that the terrorists were to learn and comprehend that in the three dimensions of our physical world, our five senses do not explain the worse than blind. At the end, they left with a form of a promise that upon getting on the other side, all things, such as getting knowledge and light and wisdom, were theirs.

Then the words ended, and once again there was silence.

When all the celestial souls were lifted from the ground, the Cosmic Master began to walk forward, and everyone else followed him in a single file. Although I was unable to see their feet, I had the distinct impression that they were walking upward, as if hiking or climbing up a very steep hill. Within seconds, literally, thousands of celestial souls had reached the heavens. Then, when at the tail end of the braided strand of golden thread, I saw family members and friends enter the celestial heavens, I felt a tug—a very sharp pull within my own heart, as if I had been connected to the braided strand of golden thread all along. Looking then at my surroundings, with all the tremendous pain I was feeling, at that particular instant, the last thing I recall is seeing and hearing the Twin Towers of New York City collapse. This I saw from afar, until I became consciously aware that I had already entered another point in space and time. When I became totally aware of my surroundings, I realized that I was connected to the braided strand of golden thread, and that the angels were depositing, or leaving, groups of Soul Spirits in certain realms of life they referred to as "spheres." The group of angels seemed to be moving us through different states of matter. Their objective was clearly twofold. Firstly, they wanted to introduce the Soul Spirits to their new or original bodies. Secondly, the angels wanted to take them to a new place in which they could spend moments focusing on perfecting themselves, as well.

With only one exception, each time we stopped at a specific sphere, a group of Soul Spirits and several angels were left behind. Before we moved on, the sphere and its reason for being was identified. As the angels spoke, I had a sense that they were aware of my presence. They spoke as though I were their pupil as well. Their behavior reminded me of I Corinthian 15:31, where Paul said, "I die daily," meaning that he was able to depart the physical form at any time, leaving it in a state of "sleep" or suspended animation, while he traveled in full consciousness and visited the spiritual planes. It was here that my consciousness first registered our departure from the first plane beyond the earth. This realization made me a better student, and I consciously began to pay attention to the smallest detail. As some of you may already know, there are many known layers of endeavor or planes of expression. These include lower astral, astral, and the first to the fourth true planes of spirit. There are seven astral planes, and each varies in density. Each plane is inhabited by Soul Spirits, and depending on the vibrations of their astral bodies, each plane becomes more refined as one climbs the ladder of progress. In turn, each of these planes has divisions called time zones, or spheres, which house Soul Spirits who belong to that period of time. In regard to the social constitution of the "spheres," growing more intense and increasing in action are six more, distinguished as the spiritual spheres. Each is divided into six circles, or societies, in which kindred spirits are united and subsist together under the law of affinity. Here, the law of attraction operates as a family relation is continued, where every member's Soul Spirit is seeking enlightenment in the same cosmic law. The law of nature, which is the supreme force called universal law, has to be obeyed in order that each sphere may be reached. Every individual remains upon the plane for which he is fitted until he subjects his will to the universal law. As he progresses, he learns new laws, but they are fundamentally the same, only they grow more intense and vital until the Soul Spirit becomes a part of the law itself.

To me, the spheres resembled concentric zones or circles of extremely fine matter encompassing the earth like girdles or belts. Each sphere had a distinct separation from the others and appeared to be regulated by fixed cosmic laws. They are absolute entities, not shapeless mental projections, and just as tangible as the planets of the solar system or the Earth plane upon which we reside. They have latitude, longitude, and atmosphere of peculiarly vitalized air. The currents were invigorating, pleasurable, soft, and undulating. The surface of the zone had a great variety of landscape, some of which was more picturesque than others. I was told that each sphere revolved with the Earth on a common axis, forming the same angle of the ecliptic. Each moves with it about the Earth's sun, yet is not dependent upon that sun for either light or heat. They do not receive a perceptible ray from that source. Their light emanations appear to come from an etheric sun, which is concentric with the Earth's sun. Finally, there is no division of time into days, weeks, months, or years, nor alteration of seasons. It is hard to understand where these spheres are, but there are many things quite as difficult of comprehension. Astronomical instruments have shown us that it is 93 millions of miles to the sun, but this really conveys nothing to the mind, because one cannot comprehend such a distance. We know that light travels at the rate of 186,000 miles/

second, but what that rate of speed is we cannot understand, for there is nothing tangible with which to compare it. Our actual knowledge of electricity, of magnetism, or even of gravitation is limited, as is our knowledge of all of nature's laws. Then, is it strange that one finds difficulty in appreciating what space is, and how it is populated?

This thought of mine is even now free and can pass through space, but it goes with its eyes closed; it hears no sound and feels no touch. However, at death, each sense is quickened, and all life that fills space is visible to the spiritual senses and tangible to spiritual touch and brain. I deduce from all of this that space must then take form, substance, and reality in a world of thought.

In respect to the second question—Where will the person go when he dies?—the answer varies for each individual depending on his mission in life, as well as other factors related to universal laws. What follows is a minute portion of the wealth of information I was given during the time I was privileged to be in the company of the many and in the presence of my Highest Cosmic Master.

1. The first sphere is generally where restitution must be made. In this lower sphere, one sees much suffering among those who are still earth-bound. Since they are busy working out critical decisions that were taken in the past, in general, most of the Soul Spirits here are heavy-hearted. In part, this is due to the fact that in the transfer our Soul Spirit does not lose any of his intelligence; neither is anything added to his understanding. So, for example, the insane pass from the earth life insane still. A Soul Spirit who has passed from the earth life insane will be cared for in the first sphere. He will be given proper treatment so that his mentality will be restored to the normal. Participations in events like wars or terrorist attacks are examples of what we need to make restitution for. In addition, any hatred, death, and destruction we build up toward the enemy affects the gross nature of our lower self, and we must suffer the consequences of that behavior. Lastly, for the ignorant and vicious, the atom

of good that has found expression in them is developed and directed.

2. The second sphere is one of instruction. It is a period of study during which the Soul Spirit gains knowledge of self and natural law. The law of attraction operates here, where a number of thoughtful men are seeking to discover the hidden forces of nature. This is where our Soul Spirit fits itself for a broader and better life. Here, they must free themselves from the burden of any wrongdoing. The goal is to dispel the darkness of any wrongdoing while in the physical body, as well as every debt due to mankind. They work with clear eyes and clear vision, and at the end, they are at peace with all.

   a) In this sphere, children are shown how to live spiritual ideals. Many are there as a result of wars. The children who die with their parents during wars enter a transitional period. They will then be reunited in the most suitable sphere for their family's progression. Other children are there because they were not loved on Earth and are now experiencing maternal love. In the physical plane we call these children "failures to thrive." When a child dies before his parents, he is taken through a process of reeducation. In this process, the child is allowed to go with a guardian to the Earth plane to keep watch over his parents' progress and when the time is right, the family is reunited.

3. In the third sphere is where our Soul Spirit begins to teach those in the lower spheres. Here, those Soul Spirits who are engineers are capable of magnetizing our rooms in the physical plane. In the process, we may hear the frequencies of their vibrations as voices. This is not an automatic process; one must ask this of them in prayer. We also find women here who when on earth never married or were married but childless for one reason or another. These women may be taking care of children, or teaching other women on the subject of motherhood. Perhaps, they would have made great mothers on this Earth plane, but as the opportunity passed them by, their desire followed them into the other life.

4. In the fourth sphere I was able to detect a partial response to the fifth question most people ask me related to death—Will all contact with loved ones be broken? In this sphere, our Soul Spirit is engaged in trial and temptation. The Soul Spirits that inhabit this sphere are capable of sensing our loving thoughts. Although it is not always possible for people to see them, they visit us, and sometimes, they leave their marks.

5. In the fifth sphere, our Soul Spirit begins to work with spiritual truth. It is here where error and falsehood are known. A person will come to this sphere if he has failed at the crucial moment and has nullified the good he could have done. We are the custodians of much knowledge. Through our investigations, we learn many things. If by reason of our position we could have done much good but failed to do so, that was a stumbling block, and before we can progress, we must become strong in whatever area we were weak. It is interesting to note that there is no progress possible in the afterlife for one occupying the position of spiritual leader on earth until he has searched out in his plane all those who had followed his teachings and has brought them to the truth. Moreover he must stand and wait until the coming of those still in the earth life in order that his error should be corrected at the earliest possible moment. To promulgate unknown or impracticable teachings while on this earth plane is a serious matter. It violates a cosmic law, thus creating a karmic debt to humanity.

6. When we reached the sixth sphere, I noticed that the Soul Spirits already there were working in harmony. None of the Soul Spirits from our groups, or any angels, were left in this sphere, and no explanation was given. I deduce from this that perhaps there were no Soul Spirits assigned to that sphere among the ones who perished that day. Or, that perhaps I did not have the required background to capture the reasons for the existence of the Sixth Sphere.

7. In the seventh sphere is where the Soul Spirit reaches the plane of exaltation and becomes one with the Great Spirit that rules

the universe. This is where an enlightened master would go to live in a condition of perfect inner light and happiness. In this sphere, the word "enlightenment" means complete awareness of all things without mental modifications. It is easier for Soul Spirits, on the seventh sphere, who have advanced to a higher, purer life to reach us than for those in any other sphere. However, spirit souls in the seventh sphere will reach us and contact us only in emergency cases—almost as when a miracle is taking place.

When we left the seventh sphere we were told that when a Soul Spirit goes from one sphere to another, he is also going through a death change. In this case, as it is in physical death, the individual is warned that the change is near and has time to put his mind into a corresponding plane of thought so that he will be prepared to meet the new life. When the time comes, he is put to sleep, with the thought dominant in his mind that he is to make the change. When this change comes, his home ceases to be among his former friends. Thought has fitted him to progress, and when the thought that held him to the previous plane has ceased, the embodiment of that Soul Spirit, which is held together by his thought, is no longer visible. At this time, one simply ceases to be an inhabitant of one sphere, and in an instant, one becomes an inhabitant of another. When the Soul Spirit awakens, he is in his new home in the next sphere. This change is not in a linear fashion but it is always for a better and higher life. The only exception is that there is no old body to bury or decay. As our Soul Spirit progresses from one sphere to another, it becomes so great and universal that we sometimes think they go beyond and must lose their personality. Because all astral matter ceases to exist on the spiritual plane and only pure spirit functions there, we often believe that they change their individuality into another form. I was surprised to find out that my assumption was not true.

As I began to digest the tremendous details of our Soul Spirits I heard a melodic voice whisper, "But there is more!"
It sounded like the voice of Victoria and I waited for more but I heard nothing. I sensed that the vision was ending and within seconds, my

conscious mind was traveling through space in a tremendously rapid manner. I felt the rush of air as if I were hurling through a vast space; and then my eyes opened as if I had awakened from a dream.

In my visual experience of the terrorist attack, which took place on September 11, 2001, was also an intensely interesting lesson about the victims and the terrorist in general. This dreamlike vision showed me many of the conditions prevailing in the afterlife. I hope that by now I have impressed upon you that the detachment of the Soul Spirit from the physical form is a natural process. This is true even when death is unexpected and or violent. However, in the case of a sudden impact, like we experienced during the September 11, 2001, terrorist attack, a higher power and his infinite mercy played a big role in the process of the death of many.

In a sudden impact such as shock, accident, catastrophe, heart attack, or suicide, in the majority of cases the entire spiritual body, including the astral-mental bodies, is thrown completely free of the physical body by the impact. In these cases, all three of the seed atoms would be separated, detached, or discharged from the physical body in a flash of a second. In any violent death, the Soul Spirit goes through some degree of shock. The deep sleep that appears to fall over the consciousness of these Soul Spirits appears to be much faster, almost at the speed of lightning. Because of this rapidity, there is no suffering or pain. The awareness is blocked from the consciousness until the Soul Spirit has been completely separated and is placed in a state of peace, before consciousness is resumed on the other side.

In reference to the victims of the terrorist attack of September 11, 2001, I learned that day that while the passing out of the old body was without pain, it is a terrible thing to drive a strong spirit from a healthy body by literally tearing it from its coverings simply because it is unnatural. Because this type of death is unnatural, the sensation following death was awful. I learned that for those victims, only through death could they progress. The personal advantages beyond the physical were greater than those in the physical plane. Since that dreamlike vision, it is clear to me that people take into the afterlife the same Soul Spirit that they had in this life, divested of the outer flesh. Everything is worked out. There is nothing left to chance. By means of psychic sight, I could perceive them so acutely that they were just as real to me as if an impression had come into my retina. I was filled with happiness because I knew that some great change had occurred. Within the terrorists, a Highest Cosmic Master had taken from them everything that they had desired to get rid of. They felt that some power had given them a delightful experience, which they had often in a measure imagined but dared scarcely to believe could be possible. It was apparent to me that the terrorists had taken a long journey and had come to a house of rest.

With no dreams to disturb their rest, they had awakened like a giant refreshed. What brought them the greatest knowledge was that they had gained what they had once believed they had lost.
In my afterthoughts of today, I can appreciate the fact that even wind may be solidified, for wind is atmosphere. All in the world is substance, and all is life. They are one and the same thing, for life has never existed and never can exist without matter. To me, the brain, for example, appears like a fine machine in constant action. In this fine machine, as a thought is formed and released, through the movement of matter they reach us. When they enter there is a definite consistency of matter in motion that passes into the brain machine. Not only can we see them enter, but although limited, we can also see them emerge instructed to do right in a way I cannot describe. If we can see this matter enter, we may understand their psychic sum total. These are cognizable to our vision by the perfect form that exists in each.

Between the two groups described above, the work of the victims was to build character. The great law that made this possible and is highest for mankind is the influence of the earth that justifies both the victims and the terrorists.
For those of you who are asking yourselves "How did this happen?" and "What does this mean?"—please believe me, I asked myself the same questions. Today almost thirteen years have passed, and at any given time, I can still isolate the tremendous pain I was feeling in my heart at that particular instant. Here is what I came up with.

How did this happen?

Well, my physical body was in the physical world, which is one of the seven subdivisions of the Seventh Cosmic Plane. From there, I left my body and went to the subdivision of the cosmic plane called the world of thoughts. It was there where I toyed with the idea that my family members and friends were dead. Then I passed unto, or arrived at, the second cosmic plane where I had the dreamlike vision while still awake. It was here where I realized, and was able to confirm, that family members and friends had made their transition to the next planes of life. This means that I was conscious that even though my bodies were in different cosmic planes, they were well- aligned and in perfect harmony.

All of this—that is to say, the dreamlike vision I experienced—was like looking at the recording of a part of a story that had taken place sometime in the past…a cinematographic story…a movie of something that had already occurred. I had the great honor of observing what had taken place in the aforementioned cosmic planes. I saw what took place there prior to its taking place in the physical world. The collapse of the Twin Towers was the ending of the movie.

I also saw the magnificent orchestration of the movie. When something happens in the physical plane, it is because it has already occurred in the spiritual cosmic planes. The physical hour or time is only a point of reference for us humans. In order for something to manifest in our physical world, that something must be complete and in harmony with the other worlds and must have taken place in the spiritual cosmic planes. Hence, the event took place in the second cosmic plane, and the collapse of the Twin Towers was the end of the story.

What does this mean?

For me this experience illustrates the idea that:
- ❖ We are never, ever, alone; our Highest Cosmic Master is always with us.

- ❖ For those victims, physical death took place prior to the terrorist attack. Perhaps it is so with every physical death of this type.
- ❖ In this physical plane, we are connected by the relationship labels we give ourselves. But in the spiritual plane, we are all one. We are all one, connected by a long braided strand of golden thread. We may identify ourselves as: "the father of," "the mother of," "the brother of," "the sister of," "the uncle, aunt, nephew, niece of," or simply the friend of someone. But more importantly, we are citizens of a point in space of the universe.

Please let us not forget that "from Spirit comes the Light." Yes! Indeed, from Spirit comes the Light. If we do forget that from "Spirit Comes the Light," we will begin to engage in minutiae. If you understand this, if you truly understand this concept, you will begin to realize or grasp the pettiness of bickering over a flag of any nation at a time like this.

The victims who perished along with our family members and friends, on September 11, 2001 were not just Americans. Many were non-American citizens from several countries outside the United States. They were from countries like Israel, India, Africa, the Dominican Republic, and Italy, just to name a few. Some of these people were legally here performing a task for their own countries. They were someone's mother, father, brother, sister, cousin, or perhaps simply someone's friend. The fact that we may not have known them does not mean that we were not related. It means only that we have to search deeper within ourselves for that braided strand of golden thread. Since this brutal terrorist attack, I have received hundreds of letters and electronic mails from across the world expressing support and solidarity. It was interesting to note that they all depicted the intense emotion that I was feeling on my birthday, on September 11, 2001. Those letters resonated in unison with the fact that we are all citizens of the world. Many of the people who wrote stated that they had included the victims, their family members, their significant others, as well as all of humanity in their prayers. While many others have expressed what had dared to happen on our planet, the tremendous depth of each writer tells me that there is still hope for all of us. Their genuine loving care and their kind, heartfelt good wishes, both on a personal level and a collective level, tells me that the writers are all "walking their talk" and their souls are in unison with all the celestial souls that perished on my birthday—September 11, 2001.

Someone once said that if we are to believe that death does not mean annihilation but only the shifting of the consciousness to other spheres, then whether we live or die is not of great concern. Nevertheless, when our Soul Spirit has traveled through the years of childhood, youth, adulthood, and are really beginning to gain experience, then the longer we can prolong the time of experience, the more we may gain and the more service we can display to our fellowman, thus making this physical world a richer world for all of humanity.

As human beings, we are ignorant of how to live in this physical plane. In many areas of endeavor, we have not learned how to prepare for spiritual birth or physical death. Nor do we yet appreciate or understand the duties and responsibilities that rest upon the individual and his relationship to society or to his self.
So how can we live here, now, and beyond with our Highest Cosmic Master?

1. We first have to cultivate sensitivity to value, which enables us to assess by our Highest Cosmic Master's absolute standards the undertones of our daily living. We must discern unerringly that which counts most in our Highest Cosmic Master's eyes and that, which counts most in our own. This sensitivity to value requires a delicate awareness of our motives and attitudes so that we can recognize our thought habits for exactly what they are.

2. Secondly, please remember that during our transition, during the eighty-four hours after the silver cord breaks, in the journey along the pathway of judgment we go through, what is being reflected are the individuals' motives. It is not so much what a man does while on earth but the reason why he did it. The evil that a man does is not as important as the motive that caused

him to do it. For the motive is in the built-in innate character reflection. The Soul Spirit cannot ascend in his upwards flight until the clearing has been completed. In addition, the judge is the Soul Spirit itself, held captive to its own thought-forms of evil.

Thirdly, we have two seed atoms working for our free will and a destiny of our own making and our own choosing. Let me explain. If, for example, an individual is born with a weakness of violence toward his spouse, that weakness can be found recorded in the emotional astral seed atom as an innate quality of that individual's character. In this case, we can safely say that this seed atom is the record of that individual's desires as well as the record of his emotional life. We can say this because that seed atom pours its atomic particles into the bloodstream of the individual, and its influence is carried into the endocrine glandular system. With this in mind, the point I am trying to drive home, in here, is that the astral seed atom is the sum total of that individual's emotional qualities. These have been accumulated through the ages of that individual's past. If this is true, I'm sure you will all agree with me that the astral seed atom concerns the present and future of man. Another point to drive home is that it is a seed atom that can be changed in quality at any present moment by the efforts of the individual.

So…how can we use this knowledge to live here, now, and beyond with our Highest Cosmic Master? Well, let's go back.
First, let us go back and ask ourselves: What is an emotion? An emotion is just a thought, and a thought can be changed. So going back to the example I gave you earlier, a person with a weakness of violence toward his spouse needs to ask himself the following question: "What are the basic patterns of thought in my consciousness that have created this condition?" Once he find an answer to this question and can pinpoint the patterns in his life that have created the condition, he can begin to change those basic innate thoughts.

As stated earlier, the heart seed atom contains a record of a person's past. This seed atom holds him very tied to his karmic past destiny and his "fate." Yes! We can overcome the past within the heart seed atom, but it requires spiritual powers beyond the evolution of the common man. In order to do this, one must make the influence of his daily life so powerful for good that it will offset the influence of the physical heart seed atom as it empties its vibratory essences into our bloodstream, thereby making null and void its effects upon the glandular system. The so called "karma of the past" must be so overcome by the powerful charges of the record of the present, pouring from the mental-astral atoms, that it cannot take root in your life and will lose its power to injure you or cause you distress of any kind. In particular, the learning of truth becomes fuel for your mind, taking you into states of rapture. The experiences we have in life leave an impression on the unconscious mind. These impressions become reality here because our minds inflict the measures of our thoughts on us.

This dreamlike vision was the first time The Tingling allowed me to experience the healing of a historical event during and after the periods of darkness. It is clear to me that if we do not live as we should, the day of death will find us in bondage, bound by shackles of our own making, because the manacles we are accustomed to on earth are not nearly as binding as the one we have after death. Many tasks will be disagreeable and not to our liking, but they will be the very tasks we will need to perform. I hope each one of you follows where the light of spiritual guidance beckons and does the things you find to do upon the way. When you are able to see and know the conditions of the Soul Spirit in the spiritual spheres, you will understand how important it is for people to be enlightened upon this subject while they are still upon earth. I hope all of you reach the time when the seed atom in your heart will exude nothing but excellence into the bloodstream. A time when the picture images released into the bloodstream, and send from there to influence the glands, will be a constant stream of purified, strongly charged particles of life, love, and divine energy.
And now to end this chapter on the topic of death and dying, let me introduce a little bit of fact and also relate to you a story of an African tribe. In my search for factual information related to this topic, I found that in a recent medical research done by neurologist Oliver Sacks, MD, he suggested that sound stimulates the release of various endorphins

and is a tool of great power in many neurological disorders such as Parkinson's disease and Alzheimer's disease because of its unique capacity to reorganize damaged cerebral function. This leads me to a story of a certain African tribe entitled Your Song: Lessons from an African Tribe. An excerpt from that story follows.

"When a woman of the Himba African tribe knows she is pregnant, she goes out into the wilderness with a few friends and together they pray and meditate until they hear "The song of the child." They recognize that every Soul Spirit has its own vibration that expresses its unique flavor and purpose. When all the women attune to the song, they sing it out loud. Then they return to the tribe and teach it to everyone else.

"When the child is born, the community gathers and sings the child's song. Later when the child enters education, the village gathers and chants the child's song. When the child passes through the initiation to adulthood, the people again come together and sing. At the time of marriage, the person hears her or his song again.

"Finally, when the Soul Spirit is about to pass on from this world, the family and friends gather at the person's bed, just as they did at their birth, and they sing the person to the next life.

"In this African tribe, there is only one other occasion upon which the villagers sing to the child. If at any time during his or her life, the person commits a crime or aberrant social act, the individual is called to the center of the village and the people in the community form a circle around them, then they sing their song to them. "The tribe recognizes that the correction for antisocial behavior is not punishment; it is love and remembrance of identity. When you recognize your own song, you have no desire or need to do anything that would hurt another.

"A friend is someone who knows your song and sings it to you when you have forgotten it. Those who love you are not fooled by mistakes you have made or dark images you hold about yourself. They remember your beauty when you feel ugly; your wholeness when you are broken; your innocence when you feel guilty; and your purpose when you are confused. You may not have grown up in an African tribe that sings your song to you at crucial life transitions, but life is always reminding you when you are in tune with yourself and when you are not. When you feel good, what you are doing matches your song, and when you feel awful, it doesn't. In the end, we shall all recognize our song and sing it well." Attributed to: Tolba Phanem, African poet, in the Parenting, Spirit, heart and soul issue of June 15, 2012

I hope you can learn today the qualities and habits of reality as well as that your lives expand into other lives. We get to know them only if we are sufficiently humble to welcome them and sufficiently generous to pay the price repeatedly. It is accomplished through practical and concrete living. We should not wait vacantly for something to happen to us by the Grace of God. But we are to seek the Grace of God by living, thinking, adventuring, and praying in a definite and practical way. Thus, the light that resides in every man as he comes into this world gradually flares into a flame that guides his life. When we pass on, our lives on the other planes are not a vague aura of loving kindness but are the focus of all our energies, capacities, thoughts, imagination, and desires.

"As above, so below," we will live in the spiritual plane as we have lived here on the physical plane. Our homes in the spiritual planes are the abiding places of our Soul Spirit who gather into it the objects of beauty he loves, and in there our harmonious Soul Spirit comes and goes, as you do in this physical plane or earth life. These homes are as real there in that spiritual plane as yours are to you here in the physical plane. The only wealth that a man carries beyond the grave is what he gives away before he reaches the grave. Please let us be wise. Let us start to build our new homes in the spiritual planes by perfecting our way of thinking and by undoing wrong on earth and also by helping others to do the same. As the story of the African tribe says, "In the end, we shall all recognize our song and sing it well. You may feel a little warble at the moment, but so have all the great singers. Just keep singing and you'll find your way home."

This concludes this chapter on the topic of death and dying. Thank you, most kindly for your divine presence. May the light that comes from Spirit be with you today; and always. God Bless!

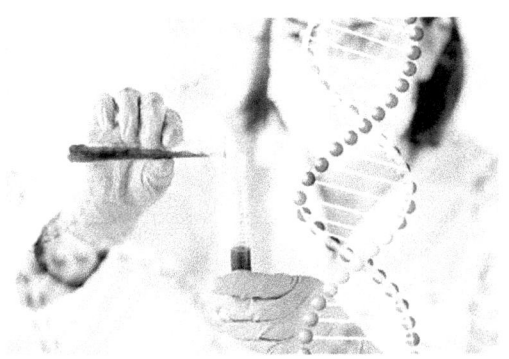

THE VEHICLE OF THE EGO

We must think things, not words, or at least we must constantly translate our words into the facts for which they stand, if we are to keep to the real and the true.

—Oliver Wendell Holmes

Within my working and educational experiences is a most rewarding one that taught me how our physical body is used as a vehicle for the ego. This physical experience begins on a Thursday when I was drawing a picture of what I believed to be my conception of a Soul Spirit. In the previous four to five years, I had completed a research study on celestial healing and had published my findings. Although the research study had been one of my most rewarding endeavors, my search for "the Master within" was still a vivid picture of a formless range of electrical undulations whose frequencies had been lingering within and around me since I was very young.

It was on that day that I realized how these electrical undulations were affecting my life. The emanations from this formless, perfectly balanced body were in the form of etheric waves. It felt as something practically invisible, almost intangible, and highly magnetic, whose nature appeared to be composed of electronic vibrations. Most of my life had been lived in the company of these electrical undulations; yet, I had never questioned its existence or its guidance or how it seemed to form a picture in my head.

Throughout my life, I have been divinely protected and guided; in my heart, there was only a profound peace, which I felt had emanated from a Master within. I also felt an exorbitant amount of gratitude because in my practice of celestial healing I had been allowed to pass along that precious gift to others. When I looked back to those years of my life, I noticed the human struggles and how they had advanced my spiritual evolution; my physical, educational, and spiritual life had been very successful. All was well around and within me, and I felt it was time to embark on a search for the etheric waves that had enriched my life. Then, in that frame of mind, I thought of the poem entitled "Inspiration," one of my favorite poems by Henry David Thoreau.

"I hearing get who have but ears.
And sight who have but eyes before,
I moments live who lived but years,
And truth discern who knew but learning's lore.
"I hear beyond the range of sound,
I see beyond the range of sight,
New earths, and skies and seas around,
And in my day the sun doth pale his light."

Thoreau's poem called to my attention that the function of these etheric waves are the eyes used in psychic seeing. I believe that, perhaps, the impression that results from its functioning gives a sensation to our consciousness somewhat similar to that of intuition. In fact, to be able to see objects formed of vibrations, which the average human being cannot see at all, is not an easy task. It is difficult to tell whether an impression coming to us through ethereal waves is made through seeing, hearing, or in some other manner. It was in this awareness that I began to think about the experimental researches in light that were done by Albert Abraham Michelson (1852–1931). He measured the velocity of light in water and found it to be only three-fourths as great as in air, and subsequently, he became the first American scientist to receive the Nobel Prize. These reflections brought me back to a state in which I wanted to draw an image of the ethereal waves that were vividly clear inside my head, and I asked myself the following questions:

- ❖ "Can I formulate a clear graphic image for the average human being to see?"
- ❖ "Is this what an artist does when he paints a picture?"
- ❖ "Do we really need to be artistically inclined?"
- ❖ "Is it a question of having the ability, or the speed, to discern an impression coming to us through ethereal waves?"

To give these questions a response; I decided to draw a picture of what I believed to be the hierarchical structure of a soul. I drew a rough image of that mental picture and found myself sketching other details that were not part of the original image, which gave rise to other questions. Throughout the time I was producing the image, many things happened, and much information in the form of ethereal waves came to me. As the new information was grasped, I found myself sketching their corresponding details. The finished rough draft of the drawing appeared to be a complete hierarchical structure of a soul, but it seemed that my artistic abilities had more room for improvement; furthermore, all my questions remained unanswered. Not being an artist by vocation or an expert on the soul, I felt unqualified to ask for, or detect the perspective of the image I perceived in my mind or its details, so I was grateful for the glorious day and felt humbled by the experience.

Several years later, after a severe back injury and following a difficult postsurgical rehabilitation, my girlfriend, Lena, called me. When I answered the telephone, she said, "Alexandra, I have been thinking about you. I am calling to see if I can come to visit you."
"Lena, hello! How great to hear your voice." I responded.
"Do you have any plans scheduled for today?" she inquired.
"No, Lena, I have no scheduled plans for today. You're welcome to come."
"Great! I will arrive to your home within the hour," she responded.
"Fine, drive carefully," I said.

Lena was a young single mother who loved her son dearly. She worked as a real estate agent and, along with an associate, owned a business that dealt with the preparation of legal documents. She had attended most of my spiritual courses, and I had developed a friendship with her, her associate, and her friends. When she came to the house, I said:

"It is great to see you, Lena. How are you?" I asked

"I am well," she replied. "I have some time off today so I came to take you for a ride. I know of a great vegetarian deli along the way; we can stop there and chat for a while," she continued.

"The trip and food sounds delightful, but I am still somewhat unsteady on my feet," I replied.

She said, "Don't worry! You will be sitting in the car, and when you get tired of sitting, we can stop somewhere and you can stretch your legs."

I replied, "I don't know if I will be able to handle going out at this time; my back is still flaring up."

"Oh…let's go!" she said with some sadness. "It's a beautiful day. I have some time off today, and I want to spend it with you. Besides, the fresh air will be good for you," she added.

"Yes!" I agreed. "It is a beautiful day, indeed…Okay, I'm convinced, we can go for a short drive," I concluded.

That day, Lena took me to a beautiful place with a flower garden that was the entrance to a beautiful healing temple surrounded by large quiet grounds. I had visited many temples before, and most of them were as beautiful and peaceful as this one. This was the healing temple of an international mystical organization. After she told me how she had become acquainted with the place, she strongly suggested that I stay at their guest house for a few weeks and rest. We walked to the guest house, and she introduced me to the guest house manager, Miss Hands, who welcomed me to the grounds and gave me a mini tour of the guest house and a mini lecture about the organization. I was also introduced to Nancy, the person in charge of the Esoteric Department, and was given the first lessons of their course in preliminary philosophy. Then we went to eat at a restaurant that was close by, and Lena talked about her son her work and her current life events. As she spoke, I was mesmerized by her beautiful infectious smile and the way her eyes closed almost shut when she laughed. I then focused on her auric field. It was very visible to me as she spoke. It was like a plaid mantle of different shades and hues of red. She was a strong, hardworking woman with many talents, a huge heart, and a strong desire to be of assistance to her fellowman. With every movement and gesture she made, her auric field became more translucent, and the different shades and hues of red appeared to be blending into a violet mantle that covered her entire physical frame. I was, to say the least, grateful for being allowed to have her as a friend and to be honored to see the huge presence and kindness of her Soul Spirit. When we returned home, Lena walked with me to the house. We bid each other farewell, and I told her how happy I was to be with her and how much I had enjoyed her company. She told me to call her if I needed anything and thanked me for the opportunity to spend that beautiful day with me. That night, I had a call from one of my previous nursing students who asked me to start a class in the techniques of meditation and wanted to know if I would be available to teach it. I told him about my trip with Lena and that I would be available to teach the class if he gave me at least eight weeks to recuperate from the surgery.

The following week, while recalling the trip with Lena and the beautiful and peaceful grounds of the mystical order, I examined the first lessons of the course in preliminary philosophy that I was given by Nancy in the Esoteric Department. It was almost as if I had seen those lessons before. I looked through my files and found that I had completed that course before but the mystical organization had never acknowledged my completion of the course. I called Nancy to verify the completion of the course and, although I had information pertaining to the corrector of my lessons, she had no record of my completion of the course or any record of a student with my name. Since several years had passed and there was no documentation found, she recommended taking the course again, and because I had the answers to all the lessons in that course, I decided to do so. Then I called Miss. Hands to see if there were rooms available at the guest house and reserved a room for a week. That week turned out to be several months during which I rested and later exercised by walking throughout the beautiful gardens and spacious grounds. It was at this mystical organization where I first came in contact with the hierarchical structure of a soul. Miss. Hands introduced me to the original text of the founder of the organization—a book I had never read—and I was able to purchase it there.

Among all the original written material of the founder, there was an image of the hierarchical structure of a soul. The image was almost identical to the one I described earlier. The founder's book was published in 1909; assuming that the diagram was drawn around the same time, it indicated that without seeing the diagram, I had sketched a rough duplicate almost ninety years after the founder's original. Then, as my rehabilitation progressed, I began to do volunteer work for the Esoteric Department and completed the elementary philosophy lessons I was given by the Esoteric Secretary of the mystical organization. I also made contact with several other people that were also staying at the guest house. Among those people were two members of the organization that remained my friends until their transition. During that time, I was able to teach the meditation class for my nursing student.

After working several years for this organization, I became the Esoteric Secretary of the Italian, Portuguese, and Spanish Sections of the Esoteric Department. During those years, I received many letters in which members had challenged the founder's statement that the blood in the human body is a gas. As these letters were read, I marveled at the members' ability to present a very strong argument for their position. While reading the members' letters, it was obvious, to me, that they had done a great deal of research on the topic. I also noticed that their arguments were sound and focused on the matter of the blood and its characteristics, thus indicating that these members were very knowledgeable in their field of work. The physical point of view that was chosen by the members, relating to the question of whether the human blood is or is not a gas, was a very famous one. Among the letters received were two physical ways of reading, seeing, and perhaps interpreting the founder's statement, but in topics of this nature, one can always find another view.

To define this topic in terms that all readers may understand, let us begin with the basic lectures of Albert Einstein's molecular theory. You see, in order to discuss the properties of blood we must first establish a baseline data of certain guidelines "so we must have the good sense to accept the evidence that is controvertibly proven if we want to stay in the circle of seriousness!!!" as one of the members stated. In this attempt, we will not be apt to assume something another person may not be saying.

Let us begin with the basic, established facts that will, hopefully, lead us to the definition of blood. It is said that a molecule is the smallest possible quantity of a substance, composed of two or more similar or dissimilar atoms, which exist independently and still retain the properties of the substance of which it forms a part. By this definition O_2, H_2, HCL, and H_2SO_4 are molecules. It is the rate of vibration of molecules that determines whether a substance is a solid or a fluid.

When we use the word solid, we are referring to the body of a substance that retains its form when confined in a container, or one that is not fluid. A solid retains its form because its molecules are very compact and, thus, are moving at a very slow rate of vibration. A fluid, on the other hand, is a nonsolid substance, capable of flowing. Because of this characteristic, it takes the form and shape of its container. A fluid can be liquid or gas. Liquids and gases are formless because their molecules are spaced farther apart, allowing them to move at a more rapid rate of vibration than solids. The molecules of a gas have a higher rate of vibration than those of a liquid.

With the explanation above, blood is definitely a fluid. We know from our biology classes that blood circulates in the arteries, capillaries, and veins. This also verifies that blood is a fluid. Now, of the two fluids, the next question to answer is whether blood is a liquid or a gas, which is the question the members were challenging. A Belgian chemist, Van Helmont, coined the word "gas." By his definition, a "gas" is a thin fluid capable of indefinite expansion, often convertible by compression and cold into a liquid. Air, for example, is an inelastic fluid, which by means of cold and pressure has been changed to another form.

The members had the following arguments for challenging the founder's statement that blood is a gas. The argument given by the members is that arterial blood gas analysis provides objective determination of the following:

1. Arterial blood oxygenation—the amount of oxygen (O_2) and carbon dioxide (CO_2) present in arterial blood, as well as the pH of the blood.
2. The adequacy of gas exchange—the means of assessing the adequacy of alveolar ventilation. This helps to assess the acid-base balance status in the body; whether acidosis or alkalosis is present and to what degree.

However, what follows is not mentioned in their arguments, and I believe it is pertinent to keep in mind that until the blood sample is analyzed the following precautions are taken:

1. The syringe is capped after obtaining the blood sample to prevent contact with room air.
2. The container is placed in an ice-water container because the lower temperature reduces metabolism and minimizes the alteration of the true value of oxygen (O_2), carbon dioxide (CO_2) and pH.
3. The blood gas analysis should be done as soon as possible since gas tension and pH can change rapidly.
4. When the laboratory results are evaluated the measurements of the patient's temperature and respirations are taken into consideration. If you take a close look at the bold, italic words above, you will realize that if human blood were a liquid, there would be no need for these precautions, because a liquid is not capable of indefinite expansion.

Some members stated that the exchange of O_2 and CO_2 is between alveolar air and pulmonary capillary blood and that it occurs by gaseous diffusion. These members are correct. This is a known fact from our biology classes; however, at this point, I must add that blood gases are not always collected from arterial blood.

Depending upon the purpose of the blood gas analysis, the gases of venous blood can also be collected and analyzed. Arterial blood is that which has been oxygenated in the lungs, is of a red bright color, and is found in the pulmonary veins, left side of the heart and the arteries, while venous blood is that charged with waste materials, which has passed through the tissues (systemic capillaries) and given up a proportion of its oxygen content. Furthermore, blood consists of plasma and serum. Plasma is the fluid portions of the blood in which there are numerous cells: the erythrocytes, leukocytes, the platelets, and hemoconia (small fragments of red cells). These elements are physically suspended in the plasma, not dissolved "physically" in it. The blood plasma differs from the blood serum chiefly in the fact that it contains fibrinogen.

As I recall, one member described very well the change of acoustic signal of the cardiac ecodoppler and presented the following argument: "While N_2 (or any other inert gas) leaves the body only across the sanguineous circulation and the lungs, in the opposite way it used to come." This member is also correct. Nitrogen (N_2) is a gaseous element that forms about 77 parts by weight of the atmosphere. In the human body, it is excreted in the urine as urea, amino acids, uric acid, etc. When found in the urine, each gram of urinary nitrogen indicates the breakdown in the body of 6.25 grams of protein catabolysed. About one-half of the nonprotein nitrogen in the blood is contained in the urea molecule; hence the weight of the urea in the blood plasma is just about the same as that of the total non-protein nitrogen. The undermined nitrogen is the one that can be directly estimated; in the blood it amounts to about 25 mg per 100 cc. This information refers to the argument the members had relating to the question: "How is the urine formed, given that the kidneys filter the blood?" This question will be addressed when the reader has additional information.

Let us now explore the not-so-common spiritual side of the question of whether blood is or is not a gas. I know that this is not the viewpoint our members chose as the basis for their arguments. Nevertheless, it must be addressed, because I strongly sense this is the platform the founder of the organization used for the teachings, "so we must have the good sense to accept the evidence that is controvertibly proven if we want to stay in the circle of seriousness!"

One of the statements most frequently made by many of our members was: "If blood were a gas it would be seen." This idea is critical to the spiritual side of the founder's statement. Aristotle was the first to mention that there was some relationship between color and sound. He believed that the colors in our consciousness created a sensation of sounds or that sounds passing through our ears and reaching the color consciousness produced colors. The technical term for this relationship is known as sythesthesia. The consciousness of sound seems to be closely related to our consciousness of seeing color, and consciousness of color seems to be related very closely to our consciousness of sound. We know that the difference in color is due to the differences in vibrations. It is this difference in vibration that propelled me to ask the following questions:

1. "But what causes the difference in vibrations?"
2. "Is this the same difference in the speed of vibrations that we find in the molecules of solids, fluids, and gases?"
3. "Why is it that a beam of white sunlight contains so many colors and blends of color, and yet our eyes do not see those colors unless a prism separates them?"
4. "Is this the same condition, the same human handicap, or the same not-yet- discovered gift that prevents us from seeing the blood as a gas?"

In one of his books, the founder of the mystical organization addresses the challenge "if blood were a gas it would be seen" by stating:

- "It is easily demonstrated that the life is in the blood, for while we may sometimes with impunity amputate an arm or limb, we cannot deplete the body of blood without also killing it. Thus the blood is the particular vehicle of the Ego, and as in the past aeons of development we have crystallized matter in order to form our dense body, so also it is destined that now we must etherealize our vehicles in order that we may lift ourselves and the world out of the realm of materiality and into the spiritual. Naturally, therefore, the Ego aims first to make the blood gaseous, and to the spiritual sight, this red enucleated blood is not a fluid, but a gas. It is not argument against this assertion that the moment we prick our skin the blood comes out as a liquid. The moment we open up the try-cock of a steam boiler the gas also condenses into a liquid, but if we make a model steam engine of glass and look at the way steam works there we shall see only the piston move backward and forward, driven by an invisible agent, live steam. Similarly as the live steam direct from the boiler is invisible and gaseous, so also the live blood in the human body is a gas, and the higher the state of development of any given Ego, the more ethereal it is able to make the blood. When by the vital processes, food has reached this highest alchemical state, the process of condensation begins, and the blood-gas is formed into tissue in the various organs to replace what has been wasted or destroyed by the activities of the body.

Apparently, this condition is not exclusively found in the blood. In another book, the author also states:

- The spinal canal, contrary to the ideas of anatomists, is not filled with fluid, but with a gas that is like steam in that it may be condensed when exposed to the outside atmosphere, but may also be super- heated by the vibratory activity of the spirit to such an extent that it becomes a brilliant and luminous fire, the fire of purification and regeneration.

Along these lines, permit me to present another example. Physicists, in particular metallurgists, speak of metals in terms of having a characteristic, a quality, or a personality. They tell us that if you hit a metal very hard, the molecules will change their characteristics. It was this discovery that led them to the process of stabilizing nitroglycerin and creating dynamite, as well as producing Swedish steel. Striking a metal with a certain force makes the metal forget what it was supposed to do. Hitting a person with a sharp object also produces the same effect. When a person is knocked unconscious, they forget where they are and who they are. They forget what is happening, flop to the floor, and lie there, until suddenly they regain consciousness. It's the same kind of thing that happens when you pass out. With one exception, it is the same kind of thing that happens to metal. A most remarkable exception is that when a metal—a solid—is struck with a certain force, it is knocked unconscious, and it turns to liquid. Furthermore, when the metal remembers what it's supposed to be, it is different than when it was knocked unconscious. If I understand this process correctly, the metal is different because the molecules that were in agreement as metal, as they regain consciousness, bind together in a new formation, and the metal now takes on the properties of hardened steel.

"Science recognizes the fact that no two atoms in any substance touch one another, but each atom swings and vibrates at a varying rate of speed in the sea of ether which permeates all matter. It is well known also that all substances may be reduced to gas. Iron, stone, water, or whatever other substance we name is capable of being thus reduced…"

Today more and more people are in agreement that there is an intelligence that allows all things to hold together at the molecular level. To form a tree, to form a chair, to form a lamp, to form a glass that is not formed in fashion and held together depends upon a tremendous detailed discussion. It is not this author's intention to expound on this subject, but what does this mean to the average person like you and me? I believe that if we carefully observe the life forms around us, we will discover that there is something there that more than meets the eye. In my humble opinion, it is something that dons the surfaces of what meets the eye, and that exists in waveform. I fervently believe that if we give ourselves the opportunity to carefully observe the waveform, we may be blessed with the ability to interpret what we see—the idea being that if it is there in waveform, each of us can see it and interpret what we see in several forms—i.e. verbally, written, or drawn in pictures of images…just as other people can hear the sound of my voice; just as people can look with their eyes and see something around them, and detect and describe it in three-dimensional thought-forms. I hope this information is making some sense and that the reader is starting to perceive the images of the picture I am describing here. If a metal has a consciousness and has a spirit in this quantum physics concept, it also has a personality, and that also means that it is plausible for the metal to have an idea or remembrance. It may have an ability to know where it came from. This information may all be there; it may all exists in an ethereal waves form.

All this information leads me to deduce that the vehicle of the ego is the only one true blood. "When blood is placed under a microscope, it appears as a number of minute globules or discs, but when seen by the trained clairvoyant as it courses through the living body blood is found to be a gas, a spiritual essence. The heat is caused by the Ego, which is within that blood."
Because the ego exists in ethereal waves, the trained clairvoyant is able to detect its spiritual essence and, hence, describe it in three- dimensional thought-forms. By definition, it can be understood that this process has various results, but that there is a process of ethereal levels. During the process of making the blood gaseous, the vibrational frequency of the blood may increase twofold. To produce the heat, a very rapid increase in the vibrational frequency of the blood is generated by the ego and "the higher the state of development of any given Ego, the more ethereal it is able to make the blood."

When the human blood is referred to as a gas, it is to be understood that the serum and plasma as well as every element found within the blood are being referred to. It also implies that the molecules of the human blood are spaced farther apart than those of a liquid, allowing them to move at a more rapid rate of vibration. The heat is described as a cool mist that is prickly in texture. It has the qualities of a numbing sensation as it ascends throughout a body part.

It does not tend to increase our body temperature, yet it is hot to the tactile sense. The heat that is being originated by the ego is not thermal heat but electrical in nature. Its purpose is "to etherealize our vehicles in order that we may lift ourselves and the world out of the realm of materiality and into the spiritual. Naturally, therefore, the Ego aims first to make the blood gaseous."

As stated earlier, it is the rate of vibration of molecules that determines whether a substance is a solid, liquid, or gas. When the human blood is displaying its spiritual essence, it is in a gaseous form of a fluid that can be seen only in ethereal waves, but when blood goes out from the body, it detaches itself from its spiritual essence and travels as a liquid, or evaporates, causing the coagulation of the rest.

What I learned from this experience is as follows. The vibration I perceive within and around me is a level of an ethereal wave form. If the theory that "the ego exists in ethereal waves" is correct, then The Tingling is also the ego. Now, more than ever, I see that founder's literary work as a reservoir of facts, a tremendous source of knowledge. I also realize that whether it contains liquids, gases, solids, or facts, no reservoir will last forever. If we were to study its definition, a reservoir is something that should be held in reserve for an emergency, in case the usual supply is shut off.

Today this organization has a tremendous reservoir of knowledge. I am referring to the studies, research, and the accumulation of post-investigations the members and officers may have conducted. I feel the members have the obligation of adding to the reservoir of the founder for posterity. I have a suspicious feeling that the organization has members qualified in certain professions, such as the sciences, the arts, literature, law, and medicine, as well as certain areas of expertise like visible and invisible spiritual healing, who may be true initiates and can share and contribute their findings in their own professional fields with humanity. Those who have written on this topic now have a greater challenge. I now challenge them to add to the founder's reservoir by researching this topic from a spiritual viewpoint.

THE GREEN DAFFODILS

You will end up finding the Road…if first you dare to get lost.

—Tiziano Terzani

My next journey began at six in the morning after finishing my daily meditation. That day was long and full of routine, mundane tasks that I had planned to do for myself. As I recall, I was home on my summer vacation and among all the things I wanted to do, cleaning the yard around my house was the major task. I decided to clean the yard all around my house because it had been three weeks since my last cleanup, and the yard was beginning to show signs of neglect. Because the front of my home has an eastern exposure and the sun shines strongly there in the morning, I decided to start with the front yard in case the sun came out early and it became too hot for me to work outside.

That morning when I went outside, the front yard was covered with leaves, especially around the flower beds. In my eagerness to clean that area before the sun was unbearably hot, I began to work rapidly. Without giving further thought to the work itself, I instantly started to rake the leaves. When the leaves were all collected and placed in the trash bags, I continued by cleaning the front flower beds. Once I had finished the front flower beds and the leaves were raked, I noticed that the ground was very dry. Upon further inspection, I noticed that the entire yard needed water, and since there was no sprinkler system in place to accomplish two tasks at the same time, I felt the need to do it by hand. To take advantage of the weather, I decided to start the back flower beds after watering the front yard.

While working in the front of the house, I noticed that the yard was starting to look well-cared-for, and when I looked at the total area of my property line, I saw that the house looked more spacious and brighter. I also noticed that the sun was beginning to feel warm and that the front of the house was completely done. In my silence, I felt that the strategy to work rapidly around the front of the house had been a success, and that feeling of success gave me the needed boost to continue.

Then, hanging on to that feeling of success, I went to the backyard and immediately began to clean the flower beds. Within that boost of accomplishment I was feeling a tremendous surge of energy and began to enjoy the work I was doing. While cleaning the flower beds, I realized that each flower had a very delicate and intriguing nature of its own. As I felt each flower, each texture felt different to the touch. Each flower also had a specific level of tolerance and a specific bounce that appeared to convey a message. It felt as if each flower were telling me how much handling it was willing to allow. While cleaning the flower beds in the back of the house, I began to observe the day as well as my surroundings. It was a windy summer day in August, and throughout the air were the traces of summer in full bloom. The weather and the birds are among some of my many vivid recollections of that day. They gave me the feeling that I was amidst the center of an irreplaceable and glorious day.

In my mind, the details of that glorious day are still vividly recorded.

After the cleaning of the flower beds in the back of the house, the work began to necessitate less conscious effort on my part; the work appeared to be done slower. In that same slow, methodical manner, cleaning the back flower beds took on a different outlook, and I noticed the entire panorama surrounding me. During that time, I was more attuned to my immediate surroundings, and able to enjoy every move I made. The sky was full of electric white clouds with a brilliant blue background. Upon looking up at the sky, I saw that many birds were adorning the branches of my trees. Throughout the air that day was the unspoken and unmistakable chirping sound of birds. Their melodious medley of chirping sounds had a soothing, tranquil effect upon the surroundings. The trees appeared full as their leaves rustled with the boisterous and forceful wind. Halfway through working in the back of the house, the flower beds felt almost endless, and I suddenly remembered that I did not have breakfast. Feeling I had accomplished a great deal of work was enough motivation for me to stop and rest, so I decided this would be a good time to stop, eat, and rest.

After cleaning myself, I went inside the house through the rear entrance. Whenever I am dirty from working in the yard, I always use the rear entrance. I use the back door to the house because it leads directly to the kitchen. By doing so, I walk through fewer rooms with soiled clothing, and the inside of the house is kept cleaner. Besides, the kitchen is easier to clean since the floor covering has linoleum instead of a rug.

On my way to the kitchen, I wondered what time it was. I felt like having something hot and decided to prepare a cup of hot minestrone soup and drink it outside. When I went into the kitchen the clock on the stove top showed 11:00 a.m. I was amazed at how the time I spent outside working on the yard had passed so rapidly. It did not seem like I had worked for five straight hours. My body showed no signs of fatigue, and I felt relaxed. Taking the cup of soup, I sat to drink it at the back side of the house next to the flower beds. While drinking the soup, I thought of my son Jarrod. I wondered how he was and if he were going to come for a visit that day. Although conscious of drinking the soup, I continued to think about Jarrod. In my thoughts, he was physically well and in good spirits. So with that idea in mind, I released the thought of my son from my mind, finished drinking the cup of minestrone soup, and continued the work of cleaning the flower beds. When all the flower beds in the back of the house were finished, I collected all the cleaning tools in one area. Then I watered all the flower beds and went to the garage to put away all the cleaning tools in their respective places. Along the way to the garage, I thought of my son Jarrod, once again. This time, in a soft, melodic voice I had heard before, his name came into my mind. I distinctly heard someone softly whispering his name; I paused to listen, but all I heard was the word "Jarrod." Although I know at least six people by the name of Jarrod, I intuitively knew that whoever was whispering the name was referring to my son. Because the voice was familiar, I looked around me to see if someone was there. I was alone, and there wasn't anyone around me or within hearing range. All I heard was a name, why did I know it was referring to my son? I don't know why I came to that conclusion, but I strongly felt it was about or related to him. I continued toward the garage and when all the cleaning tools were in their appropriate places I went into my house and remained there.

Once I was inside the house, I thought about the voice but could not remember where I had heard it before. I wondered then if my son was in any danger but something within me said he was fine. With that idea in mind, I released the thought of my son once again.

While I prepared the water for a bath, I decided to call him by telephone after the bath. Meanwhile, I sent him good thoughts in case he was going through some rough times. When I finished the bath and called him, he was not home. I left him a message on his answering machine and assured him that I was fine and just wanted to say hello. When I finished and looked at the clock it was 6:30 p.m., and I began to prepare dinner. That night, before I lay down to sleep, while I was preparing the clothes to wear the following day, my son and his face became very vivid in my mind. It was then when I felt that my body was beginning to swirl on its axis. It appeared to be rotating to the right and at the same time vibrating in unison, with a strong magnetic pull upwards.

At this time, I heard a sound that whispered, "You are there," and my eyes opened as if I had awakened from a dream. This voice was identical to the one I heard softly whispering the word "Jarrod," almost as if it had been uttered by the same young female. This dreamlike vision began when the image of my son's entire figure sitting in a park bench came to me clearly in my mind. He appeared to be happy, as if he had good news for me; yet in my thoughts, he had the face of a sadness one wishes to share with those whom we feel will have compassion and perhaps a kind word.

When he saw me, he stood up as if to greet me and said, "Bendición!" The greeting is one I taught him when he was a young boy. It means, "Please give me your blessing." I heard his voice very clearly and felt his presence. When I was preparing to answer him and give him my blessing, a strange thing happened—the image of his face suddenly appeared as a beautiful little girl. It occurred very quickly, and I was left with my words and my mouth wide open.

The little girl was wearing a white dress with a wide square collar. The dress was made of a fine white polished, linen material. She also wore white leather shoes with thin leather soles, the type worn by children who are already walking, and I deduced from that, that she was between one to two years of age. Her short, straight, hair was very dark like my son's, and it curved outward, adorning her round, chubby face. Her almond-shaped eyes were also dark like my son's. They shone when she looked at me, with the intensity of those eyes one sees on porcelain china dolls. Along her perfectly curved small lips was an expressionless smile. Although I sensed she was capable of speaking, she said nothing. It appeared as though she were wearing the clothes one would wear during a baptismal ceremony. As I tried to see other details, I noticed that an arm was giving me the little girl. During the gesture, the arm was extended as if to say, "Here, take her." The arm appeared to be of an adult female, but I did not see the rest of the woman's figure.

As the woman was giving me the little girl, I instinctively knew that I was to keep her. It seemed that the meeting had been preplanned, and the conditions were already agreed upon. The words in the background said "Alyssa Porter." When the little girl was handed over to me, she seemed to accept me as her family member, and I appeared to understand all the details. I attempted to accept the child, and as I extended my arms to hold her, the images disappeared. Then everything vanished into thin air, and I was once again in my bedroom, preparing the clothes to wear for the following day.

Three days later, my son Jarrod came to visit me and I told him of my vision. At the time, he was single, with no plans of getting married or starting a new family, and deduced from the vision that his next child would be a daughter. I felt that his feelings were plausible and added that perhaps that daughter would be named Alyssa.

One evening, two years later, I received a telephone call from my son Jarrod. After I answered the telephone he said, "Hi, Mom. Bendición!"
"Hi, Jarrod, God bless," I replied.
"Are you going to be home tomorrow?" he asked.
"Yes, I plan to be here tomorrow," I responded.
He said, "Good! I want you to meet my girlfriend. Both of us will have the day off tomorrow."
"Then tomorrow it is, Jarrod. I look forward to meeting your girlfriend." I replied.
After we set the day for the meeting, as well as where we would meet, he concluded the telephone conversation by asking me a question. "Mom, can you guess what her name is?"
I said, "I don't know. What is her name?"
He said, "Alyssa."
The name sparked my memory, and we began to wonder if she had been the explanation for my vision.

During the time they dated, my son appeared to be very serious about their relationship, and I began to love Alyssa. When I noticed that their relationship was strong, I wondered if my grandson would be cast aside if they were to marry and have children. I asked my son if he and Alyssa had discussed this topic. He said they had, and that my grandson would always be part of any other family he had. Two months after my grandson's sixth birthday, his father remarried. This time he married Alyssa, and along with the distinct family tie, in his father's wedding my grandson was the ring bearer. They had a beautiful wedding and a beautiful honeymoon in Hawaii. My son had selected, once again, to have a marriage, and the relationship he had with my grandson continued in the same manner and with same intensity as before.

Several years later, my daughter-in-law became pregnant, and I remembered the dreamlike vision. The thought of having a granddaughter was, for me, a very beautiful event. Every time I thought of the little girl in the vision, I saw the porcelain gaze of her almond-shaped dark-brown eyes and her beautifully round chubby face. My mind began to wonder if the baby would be like the child I had seen in the vision. Silently, the idea appealed to me, and the thoughts had an element of truth, which I felt was the reason for the vision. I had a good feeling that the baby would be close to me and that the vision was given to me in order that I could prepare for the coming of "something". As my daughter-in-law's pregnancy approached its full term, I forgot about the vision and continued to prepare for the coming of my new grandchild. Through the course of the pregnancy, the planning was giving me many good feelings along with a desire to see the grandchild. Those feelings were giving me an interesting new perspective on life, and I began to think about the pleasure another grandchild would bring to our lives. Then, my daughter-in-law gave birth to a gorgeous little girl. Her hair was very dark like my son's, and it curved outward, adorning her round, chubby face. Her almond-shaped eyes were also dark like my son's—they shone when she looked at me, with the intensity of those eyes one sees on a porcelain china doll— and along her perfectly curved small lips was an expressionless smile. A few months after the birth of my granddaughter, I had an interesting sequel to the vision. This time, I saw the continuation of the vision with as much detail. It felt like I was watching the second part of the same vision. Although I began with the second part, the vision continued as if the knowledge of the first part of the vision was still there, deeply hidden in my conscious mind. It was as if I had dreamt, lived eight years in a waking state, and returned to the same dream.

As I recall, it was a windy Thursday in September. The weather was typical for the beginning of the fall season. It was the beginning of a new school year, and I was preparing a schedule for my students' clinical rotation. The day had been full of events, and I was looking forward to the following day. When I finished the schedule, it was eight forty-five in the evening. I took a shower and proceeded to fix my materials for the following day. During this routine preparation, I sensed that the day had been eventful and full of anticipation of the new group of nursing students.

That night when I went to bed, the clock on my radio showed that it was 10:05 p.m. When I laid my head upon my pillow, I felt relaxed and blessed. I had everything I ever wanted and everything I wished for. I thought of all the things that made my life complete and thanked my Highest Power for my life, for the privilege of working one more day in the fulfillment of thy decree, and for all the blessings yet to come. In the midst of all my good thoughts, I was given an interesting sequel to my previous vision.

This time I saw my son's wife, Alyssa, standing behind a picnic table in what appeared to be a community park, with a little girl in her arms. She appeared to be waiting for me, as if the meeting had been scheduled in advance. Her face showed signs of fatigue, and she appeared to be cold and somewhat determined to complete a specific mission. The little girl was approximately one to two years of age and was held in Alyssa's arms. When Alyssa saw me, she stood up, and without greeting me, extended her arms as if to say, "Here, take her."

I extended my arms as if attempting to accept the child and hold her. Then I saw that it was the same little girl I had seen eight years prior. This time, the images did not disappear, and I found myself actually holding the little girl. In this dreamlike vision, I sensed that Alyssa was giving me the little girl to take home with me. I also sensed that between Alyssa and me, there was an understanding already in progress. It felt like the act was well understood, and in that understanding, I had nothing to clarify. I strongly felt that there was an agreement in place among us that permeated the act itself, and all I needed to know about the act had already been discussed. I stood there, holding the little girl in my arms, Alyssa just stared at me. For what appeared to be a few minutes, neither of us said anything.

Then I asked her, "How is she?"

"She is just like you," Alyssa replied.

In her words was an implied explanation that the little girl was spiritual in nature or perhaps clairvoyant. I immediately knew that I would understand the little girl very well, and felt it was my duty to take her.

The next thing I recall was asking Alyssa "Is there something I should know about her?"

"Yes!" she replied.
Then, before I had a chance to respond, Alyssa left and I was standing in the park, in front of a picnic table, holding the little girl in my arms. With a strong, poised stance, I stood there holding the little girl in my arms. Alyssa continued to walk away from us, and from then on I saw only her back. When the image of Alyssa disappeared from my visual focal range, so did the whole vision.

Once again, I was lying in my bed and I saw that my radio clock showed 10:05 p.m. For me, the most logical questions to ask are:

- Why was the vision given to me in more than one part?
- What is this vision saying?
- Where will I find the answer to this puzzle?

I believe the answers to these questions are found in the concept of fragmented thoughts. The answers will satisfy an element of the unknown, or what appears to be a missing link. Therefore, in this chapter, to answer these questions I will first explain my belief of the principle of fragmented thoughts.
The first question—Why was the vision given to me in more than one part?—is not easy to explain. The way I explain it is by saying that this is a way to understand the concept of a fragmented thought-form. This means that a complete message was given to me in pieces, and each vision represents a small part or a fragment of the entire message. The way I explain this belief is by relating it to psychology. Fragmented thought is a term\used in psychology when a client is engaged in a dialogue that has no logical signs of thought process. This means that when the patient is thinking, although the thoughts are perceived in complete pieces, what is projected by the person is missing certain details and their words do not make sense to others. In this process, what the person perceives, at any given time, may be complete but the details of that perception is only a small part of a message.
In my line of work, I have come across people whose speech was labeled "fragmented thoughts" by the medical and psychological professions. They were labeled as such because these clients had difficulty expressing

a complete, comprehensible thought. These clients had difficulty explaining what they saw. It was as if they were retaining several key fragments of what they were seeing in their minds. As a consequence, other people could not follow their thought process, and thus, they exhibited defective expression of thought by the words being spoken.

To continue along with this concept of fragmented thoughts, the answer to the second question—What is this vision saying?— had been a mystery to me. In the concept of the principle of fragmented thoughts, each vision is a part of one single thought- form. In each part is a fragment of the whole, and a piece of its total interpretation and each part is given before the prior fragment comes to pass. I was under the impression that the vision was given to me in two parts so that I had time to prepare for the event. By preparing myself for the event, I could develop a new level of awareness, in which a behavioral change would take place within me, thus allowing me to accept the event or any specific part of it. In this concept, each piece of each vision is to be held until all the pieces are received and carefully fitted into my life, before coming to a conclusion; hence, the interpretation of each vision is found after the complete message has been given. Since this is the only vision that has been given to me in more than one part, I have nothing to compare this one with. "That being so," I asked myself, "where will I find the answer to this puzzle?" and I knew that this message could be found. At this point in time, I perceived that in the vision there was a gentle reminder or perhaps an urgent call and decided to engage in the memories of that vision once again.

Two years after I had this dreamlike vision, for the first time, I saw a clue of the vision. It was at that time that I was introduced to Alyssa, my son's current wife. This clue is too small and may be subject to misinterpretation. Since that time, I have had dreamlike visions that appeared to be unrelated, and my life has continued to function as if that part did not pertain to me; however, whenever I attempted to recall this particular vision it held my interest, but afterwards, I could not figure out the message it was portraying or the point it was trying to drive home. Deep within me, I felt certain that the message of any dreamlike vision was the moral of the story that brought information to my attention so that I could learn from it and act upon it. The language, symbolic images

and interpretation of this vision were obscure, yet there was no doubt in my mind that the vision had an underlying concern for my ultimate welfare. Then I recalled a famous quote from John Keats that said: "Was it a vision, or a waking dream?
Fled is that music: —Do I wake or sleep?"
In general, a recurrent dream usually signifies an unresolved conflict, and the same dream continues to occur until we deal with the issue that had inspired it. Perhaps a recurrent dreamlike vision signifies the same thing. I began to wonder if somewhere in the back of my awareness was a message that this dreamlike vision was bringing to the forefront—a direct line to my inner world that I had to resolve. Then, as I began to ponder upon the message behind the meeting at the park, a light turned on within me and, like magic, the pieces began to fall in their proper place.

It is here where this story brought me to a very personal experience in which my world became a celestial example of my life. What I am about to divulge will be appreciated by those whose mission in this world is similar to mine. This information is specifically for those who are celestial healers in the making. I hope that I can present this to you in a manner that will touch your hearts in the same way it touched mine. It is my desire, my hope, and my intention that what was spiritually given to me can be heard and read by those Soul Spirits who are specifically searching for the information I want to share with others.

When people come into our lives, they come at a point in time to help us understand a problem. The meeting serves as a reminder that the person is a part of a problem in a common bond. For quite some time, I was unaware of the problem, but after pondering upon the content of the second fragment of this vision, I recalled Alyssa's face. Her facial affect was my clue that the problem had something to do with forgiveness. Should that be so, my immediate task was to prepare for the beginning of that long-awaited process of forgiveness.

When people are united in a common bond, the ties among them are always very strong. In this common bond, each person is a piece of every other person. Because the common bond is so strong, sometimes a person is used as a conduit in order to display the shenanigans of a few. When that common bond is lacking one or several ingredients, the bond remains, but the essence they had in common loses some of its splendor and strength. When this happens, said group can be better described as a dystopia society and may be characterized by human misery, such as squalor, oppression, and deprivation. Because I believe that these people are still part of a common bond and continue to be brothers and sisters today, this leads me to believe that I am a part of all those who have been part of and in cahoots with all the wrongdoings against me and against others. I also intuit that every dystopia society possesses another characteristic: in the midst of all these shenanigans…when all is said and done, and the party is over, the good guys always prevail in the end. When this happens, the common bond has been healed and each Soul Spirit is able to complete its terrestrial mission.

In my humble opinion, in order to allow the common bond to tie our souls to each other, we must begin by healing the ingredients that have united us. This healing process is a learning experience for all those who are composing the links of the common bond. In this process, we must begin by healing ourselves. This can be accomplished by healing that piece of us that is inside of each and every person within that common bond. With this realization came the confirmation that I was part of the bond that tied us together…I knew I had to begin that process of forgiveness. That day, after completing a forgiveness process, related to this dreamlike vision, I had a very beautiful and humbling dreamlike vision in which I saw a pathway surrounded by a deep hue of celestial blue. While observing my surroundings, I heard a female's melodic voice that said, "This is the road that leads you to whence you came."
As I continued to orient myself to those surroundings, I noticed thirty-three green daffodils. That melodic voice then said, "The road to heaven is paved by a delightful scent of green daffodils." The information that followed was very detailed, and culminated in a summary of what had been said to me. She said,

This road represents the earth years in our physical dense body that leads us to that golden wedding garment. The daffodils represent what we have chosen as our mission. Each daffodil is a lifetime of earth years, and the more daffodils along the road, the more lifetimes we have had. Each lifetime coincides with the mission we have chosen in order to return to that place from whence we came. The flower along the road is always a daffodil, to represent the spiritual welcoming of trumpets announcing that an earth visitor has returned to stay. It depicts the vibratory frequency that we have acquired in all our lifetimes in order to return from whence we came. In our physical world, the color green is a combination of yellow and blue. The yellow daffodil becomes green when we have passed through life and given ourselves the luxury of completing the process of forgiveness.

A daffodil is a plant of the genus Narcissus, having a bulbous root, long narrow leaves, and a flower with a trumpet-like corona of a deep yellow hue. The color of the daffodils we will see along this road is green. As I write this chapter, over eighteen years have passed, and there has been no additional fragment of that dreamlike vision.

ABOUT THE AUTHOR

Let us learn to let go, to not allow ourselves to be overwhelmed by the circumstances and conditions of this world. Let us constantly remember that at the heart of ourselves, as at the heart of all human beings, there forever stands a silent and watchful guardian: The Master Within.

—Christian Bernard, FRC Imperator,
The Rosicrucian Order AMORC.

Alexandra Porter is a registered nurse and a nursing instructor in the state of California. As a registered nurse, she has a life teaching credential and a life public health certificate, and she teaches all levels of nursing. She has a bachelor of science degree in nursing, a master's degree in education, and a PhD in health and human services.

Within the above experience and education, she is also a celestial healer with many years of experience in applying the laws of spiritual prayer. As a celestial healer she practices Aum Morrar healing, specializing in cell patterns of disharmony.
The teaching techniques she uses in nursing are those used in her spiritual healing courses. As a celestial healer, she gave courses in several topics of interest to spiritual seekers. Among the classes she taught are: meditation techniques of Eastern methods; body chakra system and its functions; techniques in contacting the Christ levels of the inner self; healing through prayer; Christ levels of communication; levels in the

self which communicate with the being; and fundamentals of spiritual healing. Presently, Alexandra lives in Redondo Beach, California. She is the mother of three grown children, and seven grandchildren.

Amidst the life the author was leading was a consciousness whose idyllic visions were its primary form of communication. The interpretation of her daily events, along with her psychic myths was manifested during her daily events. Her dreamlike visions played a unique role in her life. They let her envision her psychic myths and provided the arena in which the manifestation of a one-time event was to be healed. In this manner, The Tingling force had a tremendous impact upon the author, and her life became peaceful. In fact, the stories in this book came from those relationships.

Below is some background information the author gives us about herself. "I have been a celestial healer since I was very young. When I began to understand what spiritual healing really meant, I was about fifteen years of age. As I understand it, a belief exists that throughout the universe there is an electromagnetic frequency, moving at the speed of light, which has healing properties. It has been understood that the healing properties of the electromagnetic frequencies were the universal whole, and thus, could not be isolated.

"I have found in my experience in the medical profession a nontraditional medical ability to heal people not by means of drugs or surgery but by means of a personal energetic wave frequency applied to the illness. As a celestial healer, the idea to proceed toward the development of a paradigm theory of cellular patterns of disharmony revealed the actual properties of my healing frequency and in the interim I discovered a method, a process and a specific mission in life.

"The idea to proceed with the first spiritual healing study developed as my clients continued to exhibit recurrent bouts of the same complaint. The clients stated that in the interim, their complaints appeared to be healed. Numerous visits to their physicians revealed no signs of medical pathology. However, the clients felt that there was a process of disease within their bodies. The recurrent diseases manifested in clients' complaints, such as continuous temporal headaches, cloudy vision, difficulty swallowing, fluid in the ear, fullness in the stomach, and pain in the upper part of the back, just to mention a few. During the active phase of these complaints, the clients' physicians found no verifiable reason for them. Hence, they proceeded to prescribe medications to alleviate the complaints.

"The clients that I selected for this study were having recurrent bouts of specific complaints, although their bodies were free of physical and/or psychological symptoms of disease. These clients were apparently in disharmony, yet their personal physicians were unable to find any visible evidence of illness. Although the clients were unable to pinpoint their discomfort, they felt their lives were not leading a straight path. Their complaints were vague, yet they all alluded to feelings of disharmony. The client's tenacity to find the reason for their disharmony sparked a resonant chord within me, and in my attempt to alleviate their disharmony, I asked myself one question over and over again. That question was: 'Why, in the absence of physical and/or psychological symptoms, does disease continue to thrive?' To find the answer to this question initiated engaging in this type of experimentation, which has been one of my most glorious experiences along with the practice of celestial healing."

BIBLIOGRAPHY

Shakespeare, William. Macbeth. Act III, Scene IV.

Bernard, Claude. Introduction to Experimental Medicine. New York: Henry Schumann, 1949, p. 34.

Noah Webster, Webster's New Twentieth Century Dictionary: Unabridged. 2nd ed., (New York: Simon and Schuster, 1964), 321 4 Edward Mann, Vital Energy and Health. (Toronto: Hounslow Press, 1989).

Edward Mann, Vital Energy and Health, op. cit., 133.

Webster, Webster's New Twentieth Century Dictionary, op. cit., 2024.

Webster, Webster's New Twentieth Century Dictionary, op. cit., 2007.

Webster, Webster's New Twentieth Century Dictionary, op. cit., 219.

Webster, Webster's New Twentieth Century Dictionary, op. cit., 250

Webster, Webster's New Twentieth Century Dictionary, op. cit., 1861.

Ming-Dao Deng, Scholar Warrior: An Introduction To the Tao In Everyday Life. (San Francisco: Harper Collins, 1990), 321.

Kaptchuk, The Web That Has No Weaver

Daisetz Teitaro Suzuki, An Introduction to Zen Buddhism. 1st ed., (New York: Grove Weiddenfeld, 1964). p. 321.

Webster, Webster's New Twentieth Century Dictionary, op. cit., 236.

Helena P. Blavatsky, The Secret Doctrine. (London: The Theosophical Publishing House, 1888).

Blavatsky, Helena P. The Secret Doctrine, London: The Theosophical Publishing House, 1888

Chin, The Energy Within

Webster, Webster's New Twentieth Century Dictionary, op. cit., 101.

Richard McKeon, Introduction to Aristotle. (New York: Random House, 1947), 188-190.

Edmund Taylor Whittaker, A History of the Theories of Aether and Electricity. Vol. 1, (New York: Harper, 1960), 2.

Robert Maynard Hutchins, Ed., On the Revolution of the Heavenly Spheres, Trans. Charles Glenn Wallis, In Great Books of the Western World. Vol. 16, (Chicago, IL: Encyclopedia Britannica, 1952), Bk. I-IV.

Whittaker, A History of the Theories of Aether and Electricity. op. cit..

Whittaker, A History of the Theories of Aether and Electricity. op. cit., 34.

Gary Zukav, The Dancing Wu Li Masters: An Overview Of the New Physics. (New York: William Morrow, 1979), 50.

Robert Maynard Hutchins, Ed., Kepler, Epitome of Copernican Astronomy, Trans. H. A. J. Munro, In Great Books of the Western World. Vol. 12, (Chicago, IL: Encyclopedia Britannica, 1952), Bk. IV-V.

Whittaker, A History of the Theories of Aether and Electricity, op. cit., 5-9.

Zukav, The Dancing Wu Li Masters, op. cit., 50.

Whittaker, A History of the Theories of Aether and Electricity, op. cit., 17-22.

T. Birch, History of the Royal Society of London. Vol. III, 247.

Alan A. Nourse, Universe. Earth, and Atom: The Story of Physics. (New York: Harper and Row, 1969),

Whittaker, A History of the Theories of Aether and Electricity. op. cit., 22-23.

Whittaker, A History of the Theories of Aether and Electricity. op. cit., 81-84.

Whittaker, A History of the Theories of Aether and Electricity. op. cit., 319.

Francis E. Dart, Electricity and Electromagnetic Fields. (Columbus, Ohio: Charles E. Men-ill Books, 1966), 66.

Michael Faraday, Experimental Researches in Electricity. (New York: Dover Publication, 1965).

Nourse, Universe. Earth, and Atom. op. cit., 201.

Whittaker, A History of the Theories of Aether and Electricity, op. cit., 240-281.

Whittaker, A History of the Theories of Aether and Electricity, Ibid.

Von Reichenbach, C. Physico-physiological Researches On the Dynamics of Magnetism. Electricity. Heat. Light. Crystallization and Chemism. In Their Relation To Vital Force. (New York: Clinton-Hall, 1851).

Whittaker, A History of the Theories of Aether and Electricity, op. cit., 319-330.

Whittaker, A History of the Theories of Aether and Electricity, Ibid.

Nourse, Universe. Earth, and Atom. op. cit., 5-6.

Whittaker, A History of the Theories of Aether and Electricity, op. cit., 390-407.

Zukav, The Dancing Wu Li Masters, op. cit., 76.

Zukav, The Dancing Wu Li Masters, op. cit., 79.

Albert Einstein, The Evolution of Physics: The Growth of Ideas From Early Concepts to Relativity and Quanta. (New York: Simon and Schuster, 1938), 120.

Lewis, Rosicrucian Manual, op. cit..

H. Spencer Lewis, Rosicrucian Manual. Vol. 8, 27th ed., (San Jose, CA: Supreme Grand Lodge of AMORC. 1979), 190.

Lewis, Rosicrucian Manual, op. cit., 190.

Blavatsky, The Secret Doctrine, op. cit., XX

Blavatsky, The Secret Doctrine, op. cit., 40.

Blavatsky, The Secret Doctrine, op. cit., XV.

Lucretius, Nature of Things, bk. VII, p. 13 (988).

Lucretius, Nature of Things, bk. V, p. 68 (509).

Lucretius, Nature of Things, bk. VII, p. 13 (988).

Thoreau, David. 1817 – 1862. Poem entitled Inspiration, circa 1841.

Heindel, Max. The Rosicrucian Philosophy in Questions and Answers, Vol. II, The Rosicrucian Fellowship, Oceanside, CA, p. 145.

ibid

Heindel, Max. The Rosicrucian Philosophy in Questions and Answers, Vol. II. The Rosicrucian Fellowship, Oceanside, CA, p. 252.

Heindel, Max. Freemasonry and Catholicism. The Rosicrucian Fellowship, Oceanside, CA. p. 53.

Heindel, Max. The Rosicrucian Philosophy in Questions and Answers, Vol. II, The Rosicrucian Fellowship, Oceanside, CA, p. 145

Max Heindel, Rosicrucian Philosophy in Questions and Answers, Vol. II, The Rosicrucian Fellowship, Oceanside, CA, p. 145

www.ingramcontent.com/pod-product-compliance
Lightning Source LLC
Chambersburg PA
CBHW050727010526
44107CB00009B/760